THE
NEW
TOLERANCE

THE NEW TOLERANCE

How a cultural movement threatens to destroy you, your faith, and your children

JOSH McDOWELL
AND
BOB HOSTETLER

Tyndale House Publishers, Inc.
WHEATON, ILLINOIS

Library of Congress Cataloging-in-Publication Data

McDowell, Josh.
   The new tolerance : how a cultural movement threatens to destroy you, your faith, and your children / by Josh McDowell and Bob Hostetler.
     p. cm.
   Includes bibliographical references and index.
   ISBN 0-8423-7088-9 (pkb. : pbk. paper)
    1. Religious tolerance—Christianity. 2. Relativity—Controversial literature.
3. Christianity and culture—United States.   4. Child rearing—Religious aspect—
Christianity. I. Hostetler, Bob, date. II. Title
BR517.M38 1998   98-27048
261—dc21

Printed in the United States of America

04   03   02   01   00   99   98
7   6   5   4   3   2

To Dave Bellis
Your friendship cannot be too highly prized,
nor your gifts too greatly respected.

TABLE OF CONTENTS

Acknowledgments . . . ix

Chapter 1 / **A Growing Threat** . . . 1

Chapter 2 / **Two Kinds of Tolerance** . . . 11

Chapter 3 / **The Cost of Tolerance** . . . 29

Chapter 4 / **The Implications of Tolerance** . . . 53

Chapter 5 / **The Tactics of Tolerance** . . . 69

Chapter 6 / **The More Excellent Way** . . . 83

Chapter 7 / **Tolerance and Education** . . . 107

Chapter 8 / **Tolerance and Government** . . . 133

Chapter 9 / **Tolerance and Society** . . . 153

Chapter 10 / **Tolerance and the Church** . . . 173

Chapter 11 / **Shining like Stars** . . . 193

Glossary of Terms . . . 207

Endnotes . . . 209

Recommended Resources . . . 225

Index . . . 227

ACKNOWLEDGMENTS

We would like to acknowledge the following people:

Steve Brown of Ontario, Canada, who interned with me (Josh) for over a year, for his extensive research work in compiling all the documentation and sources and for his insightful analysis of postmodernism and its effect on today's culture.

Dr. David Ferguson, who reviewed the book's core message and provided invaluable counsel and advice.

Kathi Mills, for combing through the research and writing a first draft. Her insights, ability to provide practical illustrations, and work in breaking the documentation into well-compiled chapters greatly aided us in creating a final manuscript.

Beth Strawhun, for her research services.

Dave Bellis, my (Josh's) agent and resource-development coordinator for twenty-one years, for helping us develop the structure of the book and brainstorm its message and for partnering with us to maintain the message focus throughout.

Ron Beers and Ken Petersen of Tyndale House Publishers, for their encouragement and commitment to us personally. It means so much to have men and women like those of Tyndale House Publishers to stand with us.

Chapter 1

A GROWING THREAT

The Borg.

Half-human, half-machine. A highly advanced race of predators. They attack without mercy and assimilate their victims into "the Collective," a single group mind in which all individual thought, action, and personality are lost.

The Borg do not coexist with other life forms or cultures. They destroy any inferior individuals or worlds they encounter, and assimilate all others. They have no conscience. No ethic. And they will not stop until they have destroyed or assimilated all their enemies.

The Borg are fictional, of course—the ingenious creation of the minds behind the popular *Star Trek* television and movie series. But the Borg have a counterpart in contemporary culture. Chances are, it has already infected your community, your schools, your church—even your children. It may already be undermining your own faith and witness. And, if it hasn't already, it could soon begin to influence and infect the ones you love most. And it won't stop until you and your family are totally assimilated.

This real-life threat is called "the new tolerance," a simple phrase that describes a complex modern doctrine.

THE NEW TOLERANCE

For a long time, I thought I knew what people meant when they used the word *tolerance*. But I have since discovered that what the word used to mean and what it means today are two drastically different things.

Today's doctrine of tolerance (what I will call "the new tolerance") goes far beyond the dictionary's definition of *tolerance*. Webster's defines *tolerate* as "to recognize and respect [others' beliefs, practices, etc.] without sharing them," and "to bear or put up with [someone or something not especially liked]."[1] But that's not what the word means and promotes anymore, at least not to the majority of the people and institutions using it . . . and that is especially true among students.

And the *new* tolerance poses a grave danger to you and your family, as you will see in the experience of Monica and her daughter, Sherry.[2]

DIFFERENT LIFESTYLES

Monica was raised in a non-Christian but loving family, with fairly strict rules and guidelines. A good student—and, according to her parents, a "good girl"—Monica went off to college at the age of eighteen. She made excellent grades, was involved in respectable campus activities, and faithfully visited her parents during every school break. Then, in her senior year, she shared her dorm room with a glowing Christian, who patiently answered Monica's many questions until, finally, one Friday afternoon, Monica surrendered her life to Jesus Christ. She became involved in a nearby church, where she soon met and married a fine Christian man named Jack. A year later she presented her parents with their first grandchild, Sherry. Life couldn't have gotten any better.

But when Sherry became a teenager, things began to change. The signs were subtle at first, but eventually Monica and Jack had to admit that their daughter seemed to be rejecting many of their values. They were disturbed but continued to pray for Sherry and to believe she would "outgrow this phase" and return to the things they had taught her. They were relieved that, in spite of their differences with their daughter, she never got involved in the drug or alcohol scene as did many of her peers. Sherry graduated from high school with honors and went off to the same college her mother had attended. That's where she met Tony.

"You'll love him, Mom," Sherry declared on her first visit home from college. "He's so sweet—not to mention brilliant. He's already excelling in every class. Everyone respects him. And he treats me like a queen!"

Monica smiled. "I'm so happy for you," she said. "So when do we get to meet him?"

"Actually, we were hoping we could both come here for Christmas break—not for the entire two weeks, of course. We want to spend part of it with his parents too. But at least long enough that you can all get to know each other."

"That's a wonderful idea, honey. Your dad and I would love it. Just let us know ahead of time which days you'll be here, and I'll have the guest room ready."

Sherry hesitated. "Sure, Mom. Although—" She took a deep

breath. "Well, like, is the guest room really necessary? I was thinking we could just stay in my room together."

Monica's eyes opened wide. "Don't be silly. You can't do that. It wouldn't be right."

"I thought you'd say that," Sherry responded. "I explained to Tony how you and Dad feel about that sort of thing, but I promised to talk to you about it anyway. But don't worry. We'll respect your feelings and sleep in separate rooms while we're here."

Monica's heart pounded like drums in her ears. "While you're here? What do you mean, while you're here? Are you trying to tell me that you intend to sleep together when you're not here?"

"We already do, Mom," Sherry explained patiently. "We're in love. You don't really expect us to—"

Monica interrupted. "I expect you to respect the morals and values we've taught you all your life."

"I do," Sherry countered. "That's why I agreed that we would sleep in separate rooms while we're here. But at Tony's house or at school, it's different."

Monica shook her head. "Are you trying to tell me that Tony's parents have no problem with your sleeping together at their house?"

"No, Mom, they don't. After all, not everyone shares your views on that sort of thing, you know."

Monica shook her head. "I know that," she said, wiping a tear from her cheek. "But I certainly thought you did."

Sherry moved from the rocker and sat on the couch beside her mother. "Mom, in many ways, I do share your views. You and Dad have taught me a lot. But there are some things I have to decide for myself. For you and Dad, living together before you got married would have been wrong. But I don't feel the same way. That's what I wish you could understand. You have your value system, and I have mine. The fact that they're different doesn't mean one is right and the other wrong, and it doesn't mean we can't respect each other's opinions. In fact, that's the whole point. We need to respect and honor differing value systems—yours, mine, and everyone else's—just as we honor and respect our own. Anything else would be intolerant. We can't force our values or beliefs on other people. It's just not right. Can't you please try to understand that?"

Monica stifled a sob. "I don't know, honey," she said. "I just don't know."

A WIDE GULF

Sherry had fallen prey to the new tolerance. And her poor mother was mystified by her daughter's way of thinking . . . and living. But that's just the sort of gulf the new tolerance creates between many parents and children, a gulf that often leaves parents shaking their heads and wondering where they went wrong (this gulf will be explained further in chapter 2).

Nor do the dangers of the new tolerance stop there. Even if your loved ones do not succumb to its siren song, the new tolerance still bears many dangerous, threatening implications to you, your family, and your church. It will expose you to severe criticism. It may make you legally liable in some courtrooms. It may even cost you your job.

Consider the case of Jerrold Warner. Warner, a professor at Arizona Western College in Scottsdale, Arizona, had received glowing annual reviews until he became involved in the Christian Student Union on campus. However, after he posted announcements around campus for a video entitled *America in Peril*, which was to be shown at a CSU club meeting, his department chairman demanded the removal of the posters prior to the event. Not only that, but Warner was also informed that he would no longer be permitted to host CSU meetings in his classroom without prior permission from the vice president's office, despite the fact that other faculty routinely hosted club meetings—as Warner had previously done—without such prior permission.

Nor did Warner's problems end there. In March 1995, the professor received notice that his contract would not be renewed. In effect, he had been fired.

"Before becoming identified with CSU," said James Mueller, an attorney specializing in the defense of religious liberty, "Mr. Warner's employee evaluations were extremely high, and he was rated 'above expectations.' The nonrenewal of Mr. Warner's contract appears to be directly related to his sponsorship of CSU."[3]

Why would a college professor's employment be terminated because of his support of a Christian organization? Because of a new definition of tolerance.

Or consider Beverly Schnell's case. Schnell wanted to find a tenant to help her remodel her hundred-year-old home in return for lower rent. As a Christian, she hoped to offer the job to a dependable, mature, fellow believer, so she placed a classified ad for a "mature Christian handyman."

Her ad prompted government officials to leap into action. Her simple ad was a clear case of sexual and religious discrimination, they decreed. Rather than the six or eight dollars most classified ads might cost, Beverly Schnell's ad carried an eight-*thousand*-dollar price tag—for fines and fees imposed upon her by the state bureaucracy.[4]

But this new definition of tolerance not only poses a potential threat to you; it also places your children in a perilous and possibly damaging position. You may wonder how any of the following incidents could possibly be prompted by something called "tolerance" because they seem so intolerant. But they are all directly related to the rise of the new tolerance.

Shannon Berry, a first grader at Bayshore Elementary School in Bradenton, Florida, began talking to a classmate at recess about their mutual faith in Jesus Christ. A teacher, overhearing the conversation, drew both of them aside and reprimanded them, telling them that they were "not allowed to talk about Jesus at school."[5]

A similar incident occurred in Selkirk, New York, when a third-grade teacher stopped a child from reading the Bible in her free time. The crying child was threatened and told never to bring the forbidden book to school again.[6]

Fourth grader Raymond Raines made the mistake of bowing his head over his lunch to whisper a silent prayer. That act, however, resulted in a trip to the principal's office and a warning that if he tried to pray again—even silently—he would be disciplined.[7]

Such experiences are not limited to young children, nor to those in public school. One fourteen-year-old girl ran into trouble in her parochial-school history class. The class was instructed to write a constitution for a pseudo country. The discussion turned into a debate when the girl politely objected to a suggestion that the constitution include freedom of sexual preference and maintained that sexual preference didn't deserve special mention in the constitution. Almost immediately, a classmate erupted, saying, "You're a bigot!" The teacher intervened to prevent further name-calling, but the damage had been done; that fourteen-year-old's parents had to help her cope with the undeserved label her classmate had given her.[8]

Some years ago, I asked my daughter Katie whether she feared being called any names or labeled in any way at school. I was surprised at her answer. She responded immediately that she was afraid of being called "intolerant." That label was enough to strike fear into the heart of my teenage daughter.

Christian children and teenagers in communities across North America—and around the world—are encountering and enduring such treatment on a regular basis. Why? Because of the new definition of tolerance.

Not only are you and your family at risk, but your church will face (if it hasn't already) increasing opposition and persecution as a result of this threat.

A city in Illinois passed an ordinance prohibiting home meetings (which would encompass home schooling and home churches, Bible studies, and prayer meetings) of more than three people at a time.[9]

The pastor of a church in Pennsylvania was threatened with a lawsuit by a former member who was ejected from the church because of his homosexual lifestyle.[10]

And a Pennsylvania church received a notice of public sale of the church property to pay school taxes. The church lost its tax-exempt status in 1994, when the city council revoked the tax-exempt status of all Protestant churches and nonprofit organizations.[11]

These things are not only happening now; they will likely occur with greater frequency and intensity in coming months and years because of the new definition of *tolerance*.

OMINOUS CULTURAL CHANGES

As you read these lines, the society around you is undergoing what may be the fastest, most ominous cultural change in human history, something author Dennis McCallum calls "a cultural metamorphosis, transforming every area of everyday life as it spreads through education, movies, television, and other media."[12] It is a change so vast that its implications are mind-boggling. Most frightening of all is that most Christians seem to be missing it. As a result, we may very well wake up in the not-too-distant future in a culture that is not only unreceptive but openly hostile to the church and the gospel of Jesus Christ, a culture in which those who proclaim the gospel will be labeled as bigots and fanatics, a culture in which persecution of Christians will be not only allowed but applauded. And all of it will be directly related to the "new tolerance."

"How can that possibly be?" you may well ask. "How can something called 'tolerance' create hostility? How could 'tolerance' victimize me, my children, and my church? How could a seemingly benevolent idea like that possibly result in oppression and persecution?"

The next chapter reveals the trouble with tolerance.

Two Kinds of Tolerance

From Yiddish-speaking Jews to Mandarin-speaking Chinese, immigrants arrived on the North American continent in record numbers during the nineteenth century. Many of the new arrivals spoke little or no English, and the older generation tended to cling tenaciously to the mother tongue. But the children of immigrant families often learned English quite rapidly at school, on playgrounds, and in the neighborhood.

As a result, many immigrant families were faced with a new dilemma among the many adjustments to life in the so-called New World: The children spoke a different language than the parents, a situation that sometimes resulted in confusion, stress, misunderstanding, or resentment.

A similar situation exists today. Many parents don't realize that their children are speaking a different language. To some extent this has always been true; the slang and speech of youth have baffled generation after generation of parents, from the days of Mark Twain and before. But the language differences between parent and child today are much more dangerous than youthful slang. The two languages may *sound* similar, but the words the children are speaking don't always *mean* the same as when Mom and Dad use those words. You may not realize it, but the situation may even exist in *your* home, among your own family members . . . as the following story illustrates.

MY DAD, THE BIGOT

The screen door slammed. "Hi, Mom," sixteen-year-old Matt called out, heading straight for a cabinet. "I'm starved!"

Nancy smiled. "How did your day go?" she asked.

Matt shrugged as he reached for the cookie jar. "Not bad," he answered. "Just the usual." With a fistful of cookies, he turned to walk out the kitchen door. "Gotta do some studying," he said over his shoulder. "Big test tomorrow."

"Oh?" Nancy raised her eyebrows. "What subject?"

"Humanities," he answered, turning back to face her. "We've been talking about tolerance the last few days, and just this morning Mr. Johnson announced we'd have a quiz tomorrow on what we've learned on the topic."

"Tolerance. That's nice," she said, turning back to her sink full of dirty dishes. "Let me know if you need any help."

That Saturday Nancy and her husband, Chuck, enlisted Matt for fall yard cleanup. As they raked and bagged leaves, their neighbor Jim walked over to join them.

"When you're finished there, I've got another lawn for you to rake," Jim said, smiling and nodding toward his own yard.

They all laughed as Matt shook his head. "No, thanks," he said. "One yard is plenty!"

"Seriously, Chuck," Jim said, "I was wondering if I could

borrow your leaf blower on Monday. I've got the day off, and I'm going to make it a yard-work day."

"Sure, no problem. How come you're off on Monday?"

"It's Gay Pride Day," Jim explained. "We're all getting the day off."

"You're kidding! They're shutting down your office for that gay parade?"

"Well, management is pretty sensitive to things like that these days. Of course, it's not my thing," Jim added quickly, "but I'm glad for the time off."

Chuck shook his head. "I just can't believe it. Makes you wonder what this world is coming to."

"Live and let live, that's what I say," Jim said.

Chuck raised his hands. "Oh, don't get me wrong. I'm not opposed to them personally. I just don't like them pushing their lifestyle on the rest of society, with their red ribbons and gay parades and gay-rights agenda. . . ."

"Yeah," Jim said, "but did you ever stop to think that if more people accepted them for who they are, maybe they wouldn't have to push so hard?"

"Hey, wait a minute," Chuck countered. "I didn't say I couldn't accept them as people. I just don't agree with their lifestyle. Homosexuality is wrong. We shouldn't be celebrating it, for crying out loud."

"But their lifestyle represents who they are," Jim argued. "They just want to be themselves without people judging and condemning them." He stopped and smiled. "So anyway, can I come over this evening to pick up your leaf blower?"

Chuck returned the smile and nodded. "Absolutely."

"Thanks," Jim said, turning to walk away. "See you later, then."

Jim was no sooner in the house than Chuck noticed his teenage son staring at him.

"I can't believe you, Dad," Matt said, his dark gaze bewildered and accusing.

"What?" Chuck answered. "What do you mean?"

"You're always telling me how we need to be witnesses to the people around us, that we need to set a good example of what it means to be a Christian, and then you go and talk like that to our neighbor?"

Chuck was shocked. "What are you talking about? All I said was—"

"All you said," Matt interrupted, "was that people shouldn't have the right to live and believe however they please. But isn't that what Christianity is really all about? Loving and accepting people the way they are? Isn't that what the Golden Rule says—to treat others the way you want to be treated? Don't you want to be treated with respect? Because if you do, then you need to treat other people the same way."

Chuck was flabbergasted. His son had never spoken to him this way before. "Of course I need to treat other people with respect," he said. "And I do. But that doesn't mean I need to agree with their beliefs and support their lifestyles. There is a difference, you know."

"Is there?" Matt asked. "Is there really? Can you really say you accept and respect someone if you label their beliefs wrong and call their lifestyle immoral? Think about it, Dad. It just doesn't make sense. How can you call yourself a Christian and be so intolerant? Isn't that exactly what the Bible tells us not to be?"

"You don't understand, Matt," Chuck continued. "It's not being intolerant to tell people what the Bible says about their lifestyle. You've heard me say it before, Son: 'Hate the sin, but love the sinner.' That's all I'm trying to say."

Matt shook his head. "What a cop-out, Dad. You're being totally self-righteous and judgmental. You sound just like one of those Pharisees in the Bible that Jesus was always getting mad at. If someone's lifestyle or beliefs don't line up with yours, you're right and they're wrong. If that's not being intolerant, then I don't know what is!"

Turning toward his mother, who stood open mouthed beside them, Matt declared, "I can't believe it. My own dad's a bigot!" He threw down his rake and stormed into the house.

ONE WORD, TWO MEANINGS

What caused Chuck's perplexity—and Matt's outrage—after the conversation with their neighbor? Just this: Chuck and Matt were using the same word to express two drastically different ideas. For that very reason, most Christian parents, teachers, and pastors often find themselves stymied by a failure to communicate—or to understand what their children, coworkers, school, government, and society mean when they use the word *tolerance.* And the result is not only confusion; many young people from good Christian homes, like Matt—and many adults as well—are having their very faith in the one true God undermined . . . even shattered.

Traditional Tolerance

As we mentioned in chapter 1, today's doctrine of "new tolerance" goes far beyond the traditional definition of the word.

Webster's defines *tolerate* as "to recognize and respect [others' beliefs, practices, etc.] without sharing them," and "to bear or put up with [someone or something not especially liked]."[1] This attitude is basically what Paul expressed in 1 Corinthians 13:7, when he said that love "endureth all things" (KJV).

The Bible says, "Live in harmony with one another. If it is possible, as far as it depends on you, live at peace with everyone" (Romans 12:16, 18). We are told to "accept one another, then, just as Christ accepted you, in order to bring praise to God" (Romans 15:7).

The Word of God makes it clear how Christians are to act toward each other and toward those outside the faith:

> *Be completely humble and gentle; be patient, bearing with one another in love. (Ephesians 4:2)*

> *Be kind and compassionate to one another, forgiving each other, just as in Christ God forgave you. (Ephesians 4:32)*

> *Bear with each other and forgive whatever grievances you may have against one another. Forgive as the Lord forgave you. (Colossians 3:13)*

> *Therefore, as we have opportunity, let us do good to all people, especially to those who belong to the family of believers. (Galatians 6:10)*

Traditional tolerance is perfectly compatible with such scriptural commands because the traditional understanding of *tolerance* has meant

- respecting and protecting the legitimate rights of others, even those with whom you disagree and those who are different from you. In a passive sense, traditional tolerance means "everyone has a right to his own opinion." Actively, it was traditional tolerance that enabled Christians (and others) to fight for the abolition of slavery in nineteenth-century America, to shelter Jews from Hitler's Nazis, and to be among the leaders in the early civil-rights movement in the U.S. and elsewhere.

- listening to and learning from other perspectives, cultures, and backgrounds. A Christian teen who respectfully attends a classmate's bar mitzvah is demonstrating traditional tolerance, as is a Westerner who removes her shoes upon entering a Japanese home or a high school student who listens courteously as an exchange student describes his native land, culture, and religion.

- living peaceably alongside others, in spite of differences. "Make every effort to live in peace with all men," the Bible says (Hebrews 12:14); the people of God are commanded to be peace seekers (Psalm 34:14), peace promoters (Proverbs 12:20), peacemakers (Matthew 5:9), and peace pursuers (1 Peter 3:11). This does not require you to sacrifice godly principles to achieve peace, but it does mean "as far as it depends on you, [to] live at peace with everyone" (Romans 12:18).

- accepting other people, regardless of their race, creed, nationality, or sex. After all, Jesus (though a Jew) spoke freely and respectfully to a Samaritan woman,[2] shared meals with tax collectors,[3] and even touched lepers[4] (all strict taboos for Jewish men of Jesus' day). When he was hounded by a Canaanite woman (the Canaanites were historic enemies of the Jewish people and worshiped Baal, Dagon, and other gods), Jesus commended her faith in him and healed her daughter.[5] Traditional tolerance exhibits that kind of loving acceptance of people as individuals (while not necessarily accepting their beliefs or behavior).

Traditional tolerance values, respects, and accepts the individual *without necessarily* approving of or participating in his or her beliefs or behavior. Traditional tolerance differentiates between what a person thinks or does and the person himself. But today's definition—the concept our children are being taught in schools and through the media—is vastly different.

New Tolerance

I would estimate that 80 percent of the time when you hear the word *tolerance* used outside the walls of the church today—by schoolteachers, news anchors, government officials, activists, celebrities, perhaps even by your own children—it almost *never* refers to traditional tolerance but to what we are calling *the new tolerance.*

The new tolerance may *sound* like traditional tolerance, but it is vastly different. As Stanley J. Grenz points out in his book *A Primer to Postmodernism,* this new tolerance is based on the unbiblical belief that "truth is relative to the community in which a person participates. And since there are many human communities, there are necessarily many different truths."[6]

And, as Don Closson of Probe Ministries elaborates, "Since there are multiple descriptions of reality, no one view can be true in an ultimate sense. . . . Since truth is described by language, and all language is created by humans, all truth is created by humans."[7]

Now, pay close attention here because understanding the outcome of this unbiblical reasoning is crucial. If all truth is created by humans, and all humans are "created equal" (as the

American Declaration of Independence says), then what is the logical next step? It is this: All "truth" is equal.

Fernando Savater, the Spanish philosopher, states in his recent book, *El Mito Nacionalista:*

> Tolerance . . . the doctrine in vogue, is that all opinions are equal. Each one has its point, and all should be respected or praised. That is to say, there is no rational way to discern between them.[8]

Or, as Thomas A. Helmbock, executive vice president of the national Lambda Chi Alpha fraternity, explains:

> "The definition of new . . . tolerance is that every individual's beliefs, values, lifestyle, and perception of truth claims are equal. . . . There is no hierarchy of truth. Your beliefs and my beliefs are equal, and all truth is relative."[9]

Did you catch that? The new tolerance is defined as the view that all values, beliefs, lifestyles, and truth claims are equal. In the words of Edwin J. Delattre, dean of Boston University's School of Education, the new tolerance involves "the elevation of all values and beliefs to [a position worthy of equal] respect."[10]

Even the American courts have endorsed this definition of new tolerance by declaring (in the words of Judge Danny Boggs of the U.S. Court of Appeals for the Sixth Circuit) that not only do "adherents of all faiths deserve equal rights as citizens," but "all faiths are equally valid as religions."[11]

In contrast to traditional tolerance, which asserts that everyone has an equal right to believe or say what he thinks is right, the new tolerance—the way our children are being taught to believe—says that what every individual believes or says *is* equally right, equally valid. So not only does everyone have an equal right to his beliefs, but all beliefs are equal. All values are equal. All lifestyles are equal. All truth claims are equal.

But all values, beliefs, lifestyles, and truth claims are *not* equal. As Edwin J. Delattre, writing for the Joseph & Edna Josephson Institute, says:

> [All values, beliefs, lifestyles, and truth claims do] not deserve to be respected for [their] own sake without regard to . . . content. . . . The values of the Ku Klux Klan do not deserve respect; nor of any other racial, gender, or ethnic supremacist group. Neither do we owe respect to the values and beliefs of the organized crime cartels operating in the United States. We do not owe respect to the values of countless other individuals and groups you can think of as well as I, that are ambitious for power and use it without regard to considerations of morality.[12]

The Bible makes it clear that all values, beliefs, lifestyles, and truth claims are *not* equal. It teaches that the God of the Bible is the true God (Jeremiah 10:10), that all his words are true (Psalm 119:160), and that if something is not right *in God's sight,* it is wrong (Deuteronomy 6:18). This is not just the view of Hebrew culture or Christian culture or Western culture; it is the truth, according to the God who rules over all cultures, revealed in God's Word.

LIVE AND LET LIVE?

A concerned mother sent me a brief note after I spoke on the new tolerance at a conference in her area. She wrote:

I was at a wedding in Dallas recently, and most of the people there were in their twenties. And I wanted to tell you that what you were talking about this morning in terms of tolerance was exactly what I experienced. . . .

All the young people there were . . . fine people, very well-educated people [who not only] had great jobs with great futures, but . . . were very kind, warm, loving people.

I said to my daughter, "I want you to be very honest with me because I see something here today. I see that these are good, kind, wonderful people, intelligent people, going places with their lives, and yet they're [unmarried men and women who are] living together and thinking nothing about it. They have absolutely no qualms about it. . . . What is going on?"

My daughter is twenty-four, and what she said to me shocked me. She said, "Mom, you don't understand. My generation is different from your generation. My generation is more tolerant. They say, 'Let people live the way they want to live.' We decide our own personal right and wrong, and leave everybody else alone."[13]

Such views are not the exception today, even among Christian kids. An extensive study revealed that the majority of kids (57 percent) in strong, evangelical churches already believe what the new tolerance is teaching: that what is wrong for one person is not necessarily wrong for someone else.[14] And it is getting worse: Recent research indicates that, while less than half of the people of retirement age today believe that there is "no unchanging ethical standard of right and wrong," *nearly four in five* eighteen- to thirty-four-year-olds espouse that unbiblical view.[15] It's clear that the new tolerance is gaining growing acceptance among each new generation of young people. And if you are a parent today, your children may well be in imminent danger, based on the research, of adopting the dangerous doctrine of new tolerance.

HIP HIP HOORAY?

Nor does the impact of this dangerous doctrine stop there. Since the new tolerance teaches that all beliefs, values, lifestyles, and truth claims are equal, it is not enough for you (or your children) to "live and let live." It is not enough for you to assert another person's right to believe or say what he thinks is right. It is not enough to allow another person to disagree with what you believe or do.

In order to be truly tolerant (according to the new tolerance), you must agree that another person's position is *just as valid as your own*. In order to be truly tolerant (they say), you must give your approval, your endorsement, your sincere support *to their beliefs and behaviors*.

What does this do to your child's view of truth? It undermines the very essence and meaning of absolute truth. When your child embraces the notion that accepting others with differing beliefs and lifestyles means to consider those beliefs and lifestyles equal, any notion of absolute truth—any idea that there is an objective right and wrong that applies to all people, all times, and all places—must necessarily fly out the window, so to speak. And any person who no longer believes in absolute truth will lose his or her moral compass, his or her ability to distinguish between right and wrong. And the child—or adult—who cannot distinguish right from wrong will be powerless to resist temptation and choose right.

This agenda of making all beliefs and behaviors equally valid and praiseworthy becomes clear if you listen closely to what the proponents of the new tolerance say. For example, Dr. James Banks, in his book *An Introduction to Multicultural Education,* writes:

> Multicultural education is inclusive. . . . A lot of people are on the margins of society because of their race, class, gender, or sexual orientation. Multicultural education is about bringing them to the center, making one nation from many people. . . . To do that we have to validate their experiences.[16]

Notice what that comment by Dr. Banks reveals. He talks about bringing people from "the margins of society . . . to the center," and he says that the way to do that is to "validate their experiences." He suggests that it's not enough to accept people who "are on the margins of society"; we must also validate—that is, approve, endorse, legitimize—their experiences. That means endorsing their values, beliefs, lifestyles, and truth claims, whether those involve homosexuality, abortion, misogyny, or other behaviors that might be abhorrent to you and your children.

In legislation affecting the National Endowments for the Humanities and the Arts, the U.S. Congress has even declared:

> The arts and the humanities reflect the high place accorded by the American people to the nation's rich cultural heri-

tage *and to the fostering of mutual respect for the diverse beliefs and values of all persons and groups.* [italics added][17]

Notice that Congress did not simply suggest respect for persons themselves, but for their "diverse beliefs and values," an ideal that presumably prescribes praise and endorsement for the reprehensible beliefs and values of the Ku Klux Klan as well as for many worthwhile groups seeking to promote racial harmony and reconciliation.

And a recent policy adopted by the New York State Regents also reflects the new tolerance's demand for approval and endorsement of all values, beliefs, lifestyles, and truth claims:

Each student will develop the ability to understand, respect, and accept people of different races; sex; cultural heritage; national origin; religion; and political, economic, and social background, *and their values, beliefs and attitudes.* [italics added][18]

American Federation of Teachers president Albert Shanker objected vehemently to this stated educational policy. He wrote:

Do we really want [students] to "respect and accept the values, beliefs, and attitudes" of other people, no matter what they are?

Do we want them to respect and accept the beliefs that led Chinese leaders to massacre dissenting students in Tiananmen Square? And what about the values and beliefs that allowed the Ayatollah Khomeini to pronounce a death sentence on Salman Rushdie . . . ?

Is exposing unwanted children to the elements and certain death, a custom still widely practiced in some countries in Asia and Africa, to be respected and accepted because it is part of somebody else's culture? Is female circumcision? Must we respect the custom of forcing young children in the Philippines or Thailand to work in conditions of virtual slavery? And must we look respectfully on Hitler's beliefs and actions?[19]

Apparently so. John Leo, writing in *The Washington Times,* points out the bizarre results of a system that not only forbids criticism but demands praise and approval for all values, beliefs, lifestyles, and truth claims:

> In 30 years of college teaching, Prof. Robert Simon has never met a student who denied that the Holocaust happened. What he sees increasingly, though, is worse: students who acknowledge the fact of the Holocaust but can't bring themselves to say that killing millions of people is wrong.
>
> Simon, who teaches philosophy at Hamilton College, says that 10 to 20 percent of his students are reluctant to make moral judgments—in some cases, even about the Holocaust. While these students may deplore what the Nazis did, their disapproval is expressed as a matter of taste or personal preference, not moral judgment. "Of course I dislike the Nazis," one student told him, "but who is to say they are morally wrong?"[20]

The new tolerance has created a climate in which people can no longer say that the systematic murder of six million men, women, and children is wrong! But the new tolerance's demand for praise and approval does not only affect how you and your children think; its impact will also be felt in how your children live.

For example, in the infamous Rainbow Curriculum developed in the New York City schools, first-grade teachers were instructed that they should be aware of varied family structures (specifically, gay or lesbian homes) and that "children must be taught to acknowledge the positive aspects of each type of household." John Leo, writing for *U.S. News & World Report,* pointed out that such teaching goals contributed to "a new ethic *requiring approval and endorsement*" (italics added).[21]

This demand for praise and endorsement of other people's beliefs, values, and lifestyles was revealed by a Massachusetts college that required a Bible-club leader to be "open" to the acceptance of homosexuality and all other religious beliefs before being permitted to lead the Bible club on campus. The college clearly believed that it was not enough for that Bible-club leader to "live and let live"; it also demanded that the leader exhibit *approval* for unbiblical behavior and belief.

COME ONE, COME ALL?

Like the Borg, however, who will not rest until all enemies are assimilated, the proponents of the new tolerance will not stop at approval but will press you, your children, your church, and your community until they gain your full *participation.*

For example, Stanford University's Gay and Lesbian Alliance promotes a Shorts Day each spring, during which people are exhorted to wear shorts to signal their support for the homosexual agenda.[22] The event may have the added benefit, of course, of enlisting unknowing participants who wear shorts on that particular day not because they support the Gay and Lesbian Alliance but because *students at Stanford wear shorts practically every day!*

Similarly, one residence hall at the University of Pennsylvania promotes a Gay Jeans Day, in which people are asked to "show their support for gay civil rights by wearing jeans" on that particular day. "Given that 80 percent of college students these days wear jeans every day of the year," Richard Bernstein, the author of *Dictatorship of Virtue,* questions how supporters of "gay civil rights" would be distinguished from those who wore jeans that day because it was their usual practice. Which is exactly the point, of course, because the goal of such promotions is "to set things up so that the option of doing nothing, of not participating in a political activity, [is] effectively eliminated."[23]

Or consider the case of several Ohio hospital nurses whose superiors tried to force them to participate in "therapeutic" abortion procedures, despite the nurses' protests on religious grounds.[24] Or the students at a California community college who were called "ignorant" and told to leave their physics class because they stated their belief in the scientific evidences for Creation.[25] Or the hospital employee in Texas who was ordered to undergo psychoanalysis . . . because of her "religious speech" to one of her supervisors.[26]

Such actions reveal the agenda of the new tolerance: not simple acceptance of persons who are different or who believe or behave differently, but *approval of* and *participation in* their attitudes and activities.

As the Borg mantra goes: "Resistance is futile. . . . You *will* be assimilated." But take heart; there is hope. It is possible not only to understand but also to expose and counter the insidious agenda of the new tolerance. It is possible not only to keep your children from being "assimilated" but also to instill within them a "more excellent way," a way to accept others for who they are without compromising the truth. It is possible to follow a biblical, Christlike response to a postmodern culture, as we will show in the chapters to come.

Chapter 3

THE COST OF TOLERANCE

Mr. Johnson's eyes scanned the students in his humanities class. "OK," he said. "Back to our study of tolerance. Let's do a role-play. Who wants to take the part of the atheist?"

Several hands shot up. "Kimberly," he said, "you be the atheist. Now, how about . . . Baha'i? Anybody here familiar with the Baha'i faith?"

One lone hand was raised in the back of the room. "My older brother's been into that for a while," explained a tall, blond kid in the last row.

Mr. Johnson nodded. "Randy, Baha'i. OK, Buddhist?" He turned toward Harold. "Didn't you say something once about your grandparents being Buddhist?" The young man nodded his affirmation, and Mr. Johnson went on.

"Let's see, anyone here of the Jewish faith?" No response. "How about Christian?" Along with three others, Matt raised his hand.

"OK, Matt, you're the Christian. That should do it. Let's get started."

The four who had been chosen made their way to the front

29

of the classroom as Mr. Johnson explained the situation for the role-play. "Here's the deal," he said. "The four of you have been sent as delegates to represent your particular religion at a conference on tolerance. Also represented at the conference are people of differing lifestyles. You are all four seated at a table together when one other gentleman joins you. I'll play that part. Got it?"

They nodded and took their places around a small table that had been set up in the front of the room. Then Mr. Johnson sat down with them.

"Hello," he said, introducing himself. "I'm Fred Johnson. I'm not here representing a religious group. I'm representing the local gay-and-lesbian-rights group here in town, and I'm really excited. This conference should be a big boost to us, especially right now when we're trying to get that local ordinance passed. You know, the one that prevents landlords from discriminating against us by refusing to rent to homosexual couples. The opposition says the ordinance isn't necessary since landlords rent to roommates of the same sex all the time, so who's to know if we're gay or not? But that's just the point. We don't want to have to pretend we're straight just to be able to rent an apartment. I mean, I'm proud of who I am, aren't you?"

All four heads nodded in agreement as Mr. Johnson went on. "So, what do you think about it? I mean, representing your different religious points of view, what positions will you take toward us? Do you think we should have to pretend to be ashamed of who we are just so some intolerant bigot can control who does or doesn't live in his apartments?"

Kimberly was the first to answer. "Absolutely not! After all, what right does he have to say who can live somewhere and who can't? This is supposed to be a free country, isn't it? At least, that's what it was founded on—freedom for everybody, no matter what we believe or do. As an atheist, I say we each have equal rights to live wherever we want to live and to do whatever we want to do." She glanced around the table at the others. "If somebody else's so-called god says differently, I'd sure like to know why."

Harold was the next to jump in. "I don't know a whole lot about my family's religion," he said. "But I do know this: Buddhists are very kind and gentle people, and they don't believe in violence or hatred. So there's no way we could reject you because of your lifestyle. No way." He shook his head for emphasis.

Randy agreed. "I feel the same way. The Baha'i faith teaches the unity of mankind. That means equality, right? Everybody's equal—the way we look, the way we live, the way we believe—everything. Nobody has the right to tell us how to live or what to believe or who to love, especially based on what one person or group thinks is right or wrong."

Mr. Johnson smiled. "It's nice to know I'm sitting with such an enlightened and loving group. But, Matt, you didn't tell me how you felt about the situation. I'm sure you, as a representative of the Christian religion, have an opinion."

The group waited and stared at Matt. He took a deep breath. What would he say?

What would *you* say? What would your children say? And what would happen if you—or they—disagreed with the others in the group?

Remember, the goal of the new tolerance is not only to achieve acceptance of those persons who are different or who believe or behave differently but to force all others to *approve of* and *participate in* their attitudes and activities. But what about those who refuse to follow the pied piper of the new tolerance? What happens to people who stop short of approving and participating in others' beliefs, behaviors, and lifestyles?

Such people (including you, if you are a Christian) are likely to be branded as narrow-minded bigots, fanatics, extremists, and hatemongers and subjected to public humiliation and indoctrination. Take the example of the R.A. (resident-hall assistant) at Cornell University, a "practicing Catholic," who was forced to view hard-core pornographic movies of gay and lesbian acts as part of a "sensitivity training" session in orientation. This was not an R-rated performance, the young man pointed out; "the gay movie was really triple-X." Not only was the Sunday "training" session mandatory, but the trainees were watched closely for any sign of revulsion that might indicate homophobia (which would presumably have brought further "training" or dismissal).[1]

Such people (including your children, if they try to stand for biblical standards of truth and morality) may find themselves censored and castigated, like the *nine-year-old* boy in Virginia whose summer-enrichment-program class was asked to respond to the question "What do you do when you are afraid?" The adult discussion leader told the boy that his answer—"pray"—was a nice response, but inappropriate, and therefore could not be added to the list with the other students' contributions.[2]

Such people (including your friends and fellow church members) may even be denied their First Amendment rights in the name of tolerance; they may be denied schooling, scholarships, and employment, like the winner of the Miss Illinois pageant whose scholarship money was withheld because she was a student at a *Christian* college.[3]

In short, those who don't play along in the game of the new tolerance are often made to pay . . . dearly, in many cases. As the apostle Peter warned, "They think it strange that you do not plunge with them into the same flood of dissipation, and they heap abuse on you" (1 Peter 4:4).

"But that's ridiculous!" you may well protest. "How can such cruelty and injustice be carried out in the name of *tolerance?* How can people who preach *tolerance* be guilty of such *intolerance?* It's ridiculous! It's inconsistent!"

Well, yes and no. Such inconsistencies seem totally illogical, unreasonable . . . unless you first understand something about the origins of this dangerous "gospel" of tolerance.

UNDERSTANDING THE TIMES

My father used to say that "a problem well defined is half solved." That is why it's so important to be like the men described in 1 Chronicles 12:32. The Bible says that these men, of the tribe of Issachar, "understood the times and knew what Israel should do." We need to understand the times, the cultural atmosphere in which we live, because only then can we truly know what we're dealing with—and how to respond effectively.

The rise of the new tolerance corresponds with the general disappearance of ethical theism in our culture.

Ethical theism is simply a fancy term for the belief that right and wrong are absolute, unchanging, and that they are decided (and communicated to men and women) by God. This view of truth and morality formed the basis for much of Western civilization to date, as expressed in the American Declaration of Independence: "We hold these truths to be self-evident, that all men are created equal, *that they are endowed by their Creator* with certain unalienable Rights, that among these are Life, Liberty and the pursuit of Happiness" (italics added).

What David F. Wells wrote about the prophets of the Old Testament and the apostles of the New Testament has been true for centuries in Western thought and culture:

> They had a certainty about the existence, character, and purposes of God—a certainty about his truth—that seems to have faded in the bright light of the modern world. They were convinced that God's revelation, of which they were the vehicles and custodians, was true. True in an absolute sense. It was not merely true to them; it was not merely true in their time; it was not true approximately. What God had given was true universally, absolutely, and enduringly.[4]

That, to paraphrase Walter Cronkite, is "the way it was," the way men and women thought, and what Western culture reflected. But that is no longer the case.

Modernism is the view that gradually eclipsed ethical theism, beginning way back in the Renaissance period (roughly 1300–1600) and proceeding through three other powerful periods and influences:

- The Renaissance period began in Italy in the 1300s and, over the course of the next two centuries, spread throughout Europe, lasting through the seventeenth century. The Renaissance was characterized by great strides in literature, learning, art, and architecture; it also marked a significant shift in human thought. In contrast to the Middle Ages (in which the major theme of art, literature, and philosophy was glorifying and serving God), Renaissance artists and thinkers exalted man and his abilities. This shift gave birth to a doctrine called humanism, which stressed human dignity and ability and regarded man as the center of all things, the master of his fate, the captain of his soul—an emphasis that led eventually to an unbiblical view of man and his relationship to his Creator. As this way of thinking began to take hold, men and women's dependence upon God as the source of truth and morality began to wane.

- The Enlightenment, or the Age of Reason, began in the 1600s and lasted through the next century. While the Renaissance mind acknowledged God, many Enlightenment thinkers (such as Voltaire and Descartes) claimed that if there was a God who had created the world, he had no contact with it now—which meant that men and women had to depend upon their powers of reason if they hoped to discern the truth; they could expect no help from God. Standards of right and wrong were not based on the nature and character of God; they were the products of human reasoning.

- The Industrial Revolution overlapped much of the Enlightenment period, extending from the 1700s through the 1800s. It was an explosive period of human productivity and advancement. The inventions, innovations, and improvements of the Industrial Age fueled more than factory furnaces; they stoked the fires of human confidence. The progress that men and women saw all around them encouraged them to look to themselves for hope and guidance. Man no longer felt the need to look upward (to God); he need only look inward (to himself).

- Darwinism. The furnaces of the Industrial Revolution

still blazed hot when the theories of Charles Darwin, a
former theology student, completed the seismic shift
that the Renaissance had begun. Darwin's theories presented an alternative to a theistic understanding of origins; God was no longer "needed" to explain or
understand how the world—and man—came to be.[5]

This shift in thinking had succeeded in convincing men and
women that they, not God, were the arbiters of truth and morality. Human accomplishments had made man arrogant and confident in his own abilities to create good and judge evil, creating
a way of thinking called modernism, which saw the world
through the eyes of science. Modernists placed their faith "in rationality (the ability of humans to understand their world), empiricism (the belief that knowledge can only be gained through
our senses), and in the application of rationality and empiricism
through science and technology."[6] In the eyes of modernists,
any truth that could not be observed and experienced—such as
spiritual or moral truth—was *relative* (that is, different from
person to person). Sherry was echoing modernist thought when
she told her mother (in chapter 1), "For you and Dad, living together before you got married would have been wrong. But I
don't feel the same way. That's what I wish you could understand. You have your value system and I have mine. The fact
that they're different doesn't mean one is right and the other
wrong." But just as ethical theism was supplanted by modernism, modernism has begun to give way to another philosophy.

Postmodernism. "Between 1960 and 1990," writes Stanley
J. Grenz, in his book *A Primer to Postmodernism*,[7] "postmodernism emerged as a cultural phenomenon," spurred on in many
respects by the advent of the information age. Grenz suggests

that if the factory is the symbol of the industrial age, which produced modernism, the computer is the symbol of the information age, which parallels the spread of postmodernism.

Postmodernism is complex, and its individual points are sometimes contradictory. Still, a quick overview of postmodern belief might be summarized as follows:

- Truth does not exist in any objective sense.
- Instead of "discovering" truth in a "metanarrative"—which is a story (such as the Bible) or ideology (such as Marxism) that presents a unified way of looking at philosophy, religion, art, and science—postmodernism is characterized by "incredulity toward metanarratives."[8] In other words, postmodernism rejects the idea that there exists any "grand story" that explains an individual, local story or any universal Truth by which to judge any single "truth."
- Truth—whether in science, education, or religion—is created by a specific culture or community and is "true" only in and for that culture.
- Individual persons are the product of their culture; individuality is an illusion; identity is constructed from cultural sources.
- All thinking is a "social construct." That is, what you and I regard as "truths" are simply arbitrary "beliefs we have been conditioned to accept by our society, just as others have been conditioned to accept a completely different set of beliefs."[9]
- Since human beings must use language in order to think or communicate, and words are arbitrary labels for things and ideas, there is no way "to evaluate or criticize the ideas, facts, or truths a language conveys."[10]

Table 1. An overview comparison of ethical theism, modernism, and postmodernism.

	Ethical Theism	Modernism	Postmodernism
Truth	Truth has been revealed to men and women by God.	Truth can be discerned by reason and logical augmentation.	Truth does not exist objectively; it is a product of a person's culture.
Human Identity	Humans are both spiritual and material beings, created in God's image but fallen because of sin.	Humans are rational, not spiritual, beings who can define their existence according to what their senses perceive.	Humans are primarily social beings, products of their culture and environment.
The World	God is the Creator, Preserver and Governor of his earth and has instructed humans to subdue it and care for it.	Humans can and should conquer the earth and all its mysteries.	Life on earth is fragile, and the "Enlightenment model of the human conquest of nature . . . must quickly give way to a new attitude of co-operation with the earth."[11]
Thought and Language	Reason "can disclose truth about reality, but faith and revelation are needed in addition."[12]	For answers and understanding about life and the world around us, people should rely only on rational discovery through the scientific method and reject belief in the supernatural.	Thinking is a "social construct," language is arbitrary, and there is no universal truth transcending culture.
Human Progress	Human history is not progressing but awaiting deliverance.	Human progress, through the use of science and reason, is inevitable.	Things are not getting better; besides, progress is an oppressive Western concept.

- Any system or statement that claims to be objectively true or unfavorably judges the values, beliefs, lifestyle, and truth claims of another culture is a power play, an effort by one culture to dominate other cultures.

RIDDLE ME THIS

For years I have puzzled over why, when artist Andres Serrano exhibited a crucifix, a Christian symbol, suspended in a jar of his urine, it was not only tolerated but was hailed as a work of art and funded by the National Endowment for the Arts,[13] yet to similarly display a homosexual symbol in a jar of urine would be considered intolerant and decried as a hate crime.

Or why City Hall of Jersey City, New Jersey, can officially commemorate Ramadan, the Hindu New Year, Greek Independence Day, and Dominican Flag-Raising Day (among many, many others), but (according to the ACLU and a federal court of appeals) cannot display a manger scene at Christmas.[14]

Or why Christian employees' requests to start a prayer group were repeatedly stalled by the (U.S.) Federal Aviation Administration when gay activist groups are not only allowed but encouraged by the agency.[15]

Such antagonism toward Christianity is befuddling, particularly when it is perpetrated in the guise of so-called *tolerance!* But now that we know the basic tenets of the new tolerance, we can begin to understand why Christianity and Christians will be—in fact, *must* be—the target of the new tolerance.

For example, remember Chuck's conversation with his neighbor Jim in chapter 2? The two men seemed to be speaking two different languages—which, in a way, they were, because

Chuck was operating according to traditional tolerance, while Jim was defending the new tolerance. When Chuck said, "I didn't say I couldn't accept them as people. I just don't agree with their lifestyle," he was viewing the homosexual agenda from the perspective of traditional tolerance. But that approach was intolerant, Jim argued, because "their lifestyle represents *who they are.*" That exchange between the two men points out a basic premise of postmodernism and the new tolerance: There is no difference between who a person is and that person's beliefs, behavior, culture, or lifestyle. If it were written as an equation, it would look like this:

Who I Am = What I Do

According to the new tolerance, who I am is inseparable from what I do and think and believe; my identity is wrapped up in my culture and conduct. Therefore, if you express any disagreement with my beliefs, you are disparaging *me!* If you say that my behavior is wrong, you're judging *me!* If you criticize my culture, you're criticizing *me!* If you can't accept my lifestyle, you're being intolerant of *me!* The French politician Edgard Pisani says:

> Intolerance . . . is not simply the lack of a sense of solidarity with other people: it is the rejection of others *for what they are, for what they do, for what they think and, eventually, simply because they exist.* [italics added][16]

Do you see what he is saying? He admits no possibility of accepting and respecting a person without approving and endorsing "what he does" and "what he thinks."

One educator has recognized this attitude among his students. He writes:

> For the past few years, I have asked my students to complete survey questions. . . . One such question is "Can a person's beliefs or values be criticized without being critical of the person—without attacking the person's integrity and character?" Invariably, the vast majority of the students answer "No." In the space open for optional comments, many students elaborate on their "no" answers: *"What I believe can't be separated from who I am"*; [and] *"To criticize what's important to someone is to criticize that person."* [italics added][17]

This attitude was reflected recently by the pastor of a church "that welcomes practicing homosexuals" and has ordained a homosexual deacon. When his denomination considered severing ties with the church, the pastor said, "Gays and lesbians and their families are damaged once again by hearing that God hates them." Responding to the observation that Christians should love the sinner but hate the sin, he added, "They [homosexuals] hear that the way an African American would hear, 'Love the soul and hate the color,' or a woman would hear, 'Love the woman but hate the gender.'"[18]

Do you see what that pastor was saying? He equated "who a person is" with "what a person does." He recognized no distinction between a homosexual person and homosexual behavior and, as a result, came to the conclusion that said, in effect, if you don't approve of a person's lifestyle, you don't love *the person.*

According to the definition of traditional tolerance, a person can reject another person's lifestyle and still love and accept that person as one created in the image of God, one who is deserving of respect. Scripture does not teach that what we do constitutes the whole of who we are; the Bible says that "God created man in his own image . . . male and female he created them" (Genesis 1:27). He created human beings as individuals made in his own image and with his own hands (Genesis 2:7), not just as products of their cultures and communities. Our beliefs and behavior affect us, of course. Isaiah wrote, "Your iniquities have separated you from your God" (Isaiah 59:2), but his words show a clear distinction between who we are and what we do (in this case, our iniquities). But praise God that what we do is *not* the same as who we are, for otherwise God in Christ could not have separated our sins from us and thrown them into the sea of his forgetfulness (Micah 7:18-19).

But because the new tolerance works from the false assumption that "what I do represents who I am," to accept and respect someone, *you must approve and endorse* that person's beliefs, values, and lifestyle. And, if and when you don't, you are considered insensitive, intolerant, and bigoted!

This is the assumption underlying the words of British philosopher R. M. Haire, who defines tolerance as "a readiness to respect other people's ideals as if they were [your] own."[19] Haire's idea of respect does not mean an attitude that says, "I love you, I respect you, but I disagree with your ideals"; it means an attitude that says, "Your ideals are just as valid as my own" because in the lexicon of the new tolerance, respecting *me* means accepting and approving *my ideals* . . . because "what I believe represents who I am." In other words, if you do not respect my values, my beliefs, my claim to truth, my lifestyle, as much as you do your own, then you are intolerant because you're making a value judgment on my beliefs . . . and that, according to the new tolerance, is a judgment of me as a person.

INTOLERANCE OF THE INTOLERANT

In a postmodern society—a society that regards all values, beliefs, lifestyles, and truth claims as equally valid—there can be only one universal virtue: tolerance. And, if tolerance is the cardinal virtue, the sole absolute, then there can be only one evil: *intolerance*. And that is exactly the attitude we see among the proponents of the new tolerance.

Dr. Frederick W. Hill, a school administrator, said:

It is the mission of public schools not to tolerate intolerances.[20]

Leslie Armour, a philosophy professor at the University of Ottawa, proposed:

Our idea is that to be a virtuous citizen is to be one who tolerates everything except intolerance.[21]

But what does it mean to be "intolerant," according to such people? According to the United Nations "Declaration of Principles on Tolerance,"

Tolerance . . . involves the rejection of dogmatism and absolutism.[22]

Ironic, isn't it, that the proponents of the new tolerance are so dogmatic about dogmatism and so absolute in their opposition to absolutism? Perhaps it is appropriate, however, since they are also intolerant toward "intolerance," as author Ryszard Legutko puts it in his essay, "The Trouble with Toleration":

All those who cherish the value of diversity must perceive those even merely considering the subjection of the plurality of ideals to selection and hierarchical organization to be intolerant.[23]

In other words, any system or individual that believes dogmatically in anything—and especially in absolute truth—is *by definition* guilty of intolerance! You don't even have to say anything; if you do not reject the idea that some beliefs and behaviors are right and that others are wrong, for all people, for all places, and for all times, then *you are intolerant . . . and thus you are an appropriate object of intolerance!* If you—or your church, or your children—"make *any* negative judgments about other points of view,"[24] you *will* be targeted (italics added).

That is why the proponents of the new tolerance have no problem being intolerant toward Christians, Christianity, and Christian morality—because those things present problems for the new tolerance in four basic areas:

1. Biblical truth. The truth claims and commands of the Bible are considered too narrow by today's definition of *tolerance*. Christians' belief in a "God of truth" (Isaiah 65:16) and in "the Book of Truth" (Daniel 10:21) is intolerable to the proponents of the new tolerance, who consider a belief in absolute truth to be evil and offensive. Such attitudes create an ideal climate for incidents like the following:

> In Manassas, Virginia, ten-year-old Audrey Pearson began taking her Bible with her to help pass the time on her hour-long bus ride to school. The principal said she could not bring her Bible to school. . . .[25]

2. Jesus and the cross. The claims of Jesus and the message of the cross are an affront to today's definition of tolerance.

Jesus said, "I am the way and the truth and the life. No one comes to the Father except through me" (John 14:6). The new tolerance sees such a claim as intolerably narrow and exclusionary, which helps to explain such contrasts as that which occurred recently when the city of San Jose erected a $500,000 statue of Quetzalcoatl, an Aztec god,[26] while less than a hundred miles away, a 103-foot cross in a San Francisco park was determined to be unconstitutional and was slated for destruction.[27]

Such an apparent contradiction is permitted because the Aztec god represents just one religion among many, while the cross represents the exclusive claims of Jesus and is therefore a symbol of intolerance (which also explains why, as mentioned earlier in this chapter, Andres Serrano's crucifix suspended in a jar of urine is considered art, while similar treatment of a gay symbol would be intolerance . . . because the cross represents the exclusive and intolerant claims of Jesus, and such "intolerance" must be met with intolerance).

3. Sin. Jesus told his disciples, "The world . . . hates me because I testify that what it does is evil" (John 7:7). Things have not changed much in twenty centuries, which is why today, any suggestion that "all have sinned" (Romans 3:23) and that all have need of a Savior represents an intolerable assertion according to the new tolerance, which is based upon the belief that sin is (at most) a cultural concept, one that cannot be applied to everyone. This explains the decision of the British Columbia College of Teachers (BCCT) to deny accreditation to Trinity Western University (TWU) and force the Christian school's education students to finish their degrees at a secular institution:

Central to BCCT's [decision] was one paragraph in TWU's community standards contract. The contract requires students to refrain from various activities, including "involvement in the occult, and sexual sins such as premarital sex, adultery or homosexual behavior."

Leading the charge against TWU's accreditation, according to Vancouver's *Christian Info* newspaper, was college council member Annabelle Paxton. *Christian Info* reported that Paxton, a self-declared lesbian, "took exception to mentioning dishonesty, the occult and homosexual behavior in the same sentence."

In a letter to TWU, the BCCT expressed its belief that "the proposed program follows discriminatory practices which are contrary to the public interest and public policy."[28]

In the lexicon of the new tolerance, for a religious institution to call homosexual behavior "sin" is judgmental and "discriminatory" (because it implies that all beliefs, behaviors, and lifestyles are *not* equal) and as such invites retaliation.

4. The mission of the church. The church itself likewise represents an intolerable challenge to the new tolerance. Jesus commanded his followers to "go and make disciples of all nations, baptizing them in the name of the Father and of the Son and of the Holy Spirit" (Matthew 28:19), an intolerable mission that the new tolerance necessarily defines as a fanatical effort to impose upon and dominate other cultures and other viewpoints.

Stanford University student Scott Scruggs relates:

[Recently], a dean at Stanford University began to pressure evangelical Christian groups on campus to stop the practice of "proselytizing other students." Ironically, what angered the dean was not the content of the message that was being shared, but the practice of sharing itself. He believes that in approaching someone with the Gospel, you are implying that the person's beliefs are inferior to your own. Such an implication is unacceptable because it is self-righteous, biased, and intolerant.[29]

Of course, the dean did not consider it biased or intolerant for him to "proselytize" the Christian students to his view of tolerance because in so doing he was simply stamping out the "evil" of intolerance. Nonetheless, his warning illustrates how Christians have become a target of the new tolerance because any effort to evangelize, which is the mission of the church, is an affront because it implies that the Christian gospel is "better" or "more true" than all other ideas or religions. And that view, of course, cannot be tolerated by those who espouse the new tolerance.

In fact, the nations of Brazil and Guatemala have both made it illegal for Christians to share the gospel with Native Indians, a position that has been supported and enforced by the United Nations!

THE TEMPLE OF TOLERANCE

The effect of all this is twofold: First, in an active sense, the new tolerance cannot be other than a fierce opponent of Christ, Christianity, and Christians. James Wood writes:

> The problem of tolerance has been called, in the words of Gustav Mensching, "one of the great and most urgent challenges now confronting our world." The action taken by the United Nations General Assembly, 25 November

1981, in adopting the "Declaration on the Elimination of All Forms of Intolerance and of Discrimination Based on Religion or Belief," while long overdue, was an important step taken by the family of nations.[30]

The "elimination of all forms of intolerance" by the "the family of nations" will necessarily target those of us with a message of universal truth. We, in the family of God, will increasingly find ourselves at odds with the "family of nations." But why should that surprise us? Jesus said the world hated him; he warned that it would hate us also. As long as we continue to proclaim the same absolute, exclusive message that Christ proclaimed when he walked the earth, we can expect to encounter increased persecution and "tribulation" in the world (see John 16:33) and even more so as the new tolerance continues to gain acceptance. Which helps explain why Don Argue, former president of the National Association of Evangelicals, can say, "The tragic fact is that Christians have become the special targets of religious persecution in the world today."

Second, in a more passive sense, the new tolerance serves as a modern temple of idolatry, like the Gandhi Mandapan on the south side of the city of Madras, in India:

> Carved on several of the pillars are figures or symbols of the various religions: a Christian crucifix, a meditating Buddha, a Hindu god, and Islamic calligraphy from the Koran. And on a corner pillar are the words of the Mahatma: "I came to the conclusion long ago that all religions were true, and also that all had some error in them; and that whilst I hold my own, I should hold others as dear as Hinduism."[31]

Gandhi's words, of course, pose a fatal problem,[32] but the more pertinent point is that the Temple of Tolerance, like the Gandhi Mandapan, shelters any and all religions (except those that espouse absolute standards of truth and morality, like Christianity, Orthodox Judaism, and Islam). The new tolerance becomes a gleaming temple for idols of every shape and size, which seduce you—and especially your children—by means of a deceptive and dangerous cycle.

The first step leading to this Temple of Tolerance is the undermining of a person's faith in the living God, the God of Abraham, Isaac, and Jacob. This can happen as your child is ridiculed or intimidated because of his faith, for example, or persecuted for praying to God or told that everyone's beliefs are equal to his own. Little by little, day after day, a once-strong faith in God can be eroded.

Once a person is thus induced to doubt the one true God, he or she loses the true standard for right and wrong, which is the nature and character of God himself. If our children, for example, no longer believe strongly in the God of the Bible, they are not likely to turn to him (whom they doubt) for moral guidance. Instead of comparing their actions and attitudes to God and his revelation, they will turn inward, looking to themselves for moral guidance and, in so doing, stumble into an idolatry that is as pernicious as it is prevalent, one that dates back to the dawn of time itself . . . to the Garden of Eden.

When Eve succumbed to the temptation to eat of the tree of the knowledge of good and evil (Genesis 3), she made an important decision, one that has affected generation after generation of her race. She knew that God had already decided—and communicated—what was right and what was wrong. He had clearly said, "You are free to eat from any tree in the garden; but you must not eat from the tree of the knowledge of good and evil, for when you eat of it you will surely die" (Genesis 2:16-17).

But Eve decided that wasn't good enough for her. Enticed by the serpent, she determined that she wasn't going to let God tell her what was good and what was bad; she would make that decision herself. The evil one questioned God's word and tempted her with a promise that she would "be like God, knowing good and evil" (Genesis 3:5). As Christian apologist and author Ravi Zacharias points out, when she and her husband "questioned the reality of His voice and supplanted it with their own authority, they made themselves the measure of all things."[33] They set themselves up in God's place and took something that belonged only to God: the power to decide what is good and what is evil.

That idolatry is the second step leading into the Temple of Tolerance. It is an idolatry that says, in effect, "I will be my own god. I will determine what is right or wrong, what is true or false, what is good or evil." It is the same idolatry that ruined the king of Babylon (whom some consider a type of Satan), who said, "I will ascend to heaven; I will raise my throne above the stars of God; I will sit enthroned on the mount of assembly, on the utmost heights of the sacred mountain. I will ascend above the tops of the clouds; I will make myself like the Most High" (Isaiah 14:13-14).

Once you or your child is enticed this far, the next step into the Temple of Tolerance—doing what is right in his or her own eyes—is nearly unavoidable. For it is only natural, once a person replaces God's revelation of right and wrong with a custom-made, personalized right and wrong, to put that principle into practice.

As the faith of a child—or adult—is undermined, causing

him or her to look inside (instead of to God) for moral guidance and begin doing what is right in his or her own eyes, the final step becomes unavoidable. If the testimony of the Bible—and of our own experience—teaches us anything, it is that when we do what is right in our own eyes, we will become susceptible to dangerous beliefs like New Age ideas and to destructive behaviors like sexual immorality and substance abuse.

The cycle is complete then, for a person who is engaged in sinful beliefs and behaviors will very likely feel distant, even alienated, from God . . . and the erosion of faith that began the cycle will perpetuate itself.

But there is an effective, biblical way to counter this destructive new tolerance, and we will explore it in detail. First, however, we need to fully grasp the implications of tolerance and its insidious tactics.

Chapter 4

THE IMPLICATIONS
OF TOLERANCE

Could speaking the name of Jesus get you thrown in jail?

Several years ago, Judge Samuel B. Kent of the U.S. District Court for the Southern District of Texas ruled that any student mentioning the name of Jesus in a graduation prayer would be sentenced to a six-month jail term!

The following are the judge's own words, taken directly from court papers dated May 5, 1995:

> And make no mistake, the court is going to have a
> United States marshal in attendance at the graduation. If
> any student offends this court, that student will be sum-
> marily arrested and will face up to six months incarcera-
> tion in the Galveston County Jail for contempt of court.
> Anyone who thinks I'm kidding about this order . . . [or]
> expressing any weakness or lack of resolve in that spirit
> of compromise would better think again. Anyone who
> violates these orders, no kidding, is going to wish that he
> or she had died as a child when this court gets through
> with it.[1]

The judge's words might not sound so shocking if they had been spoken in the former Soviet Union or in a despotic regime like that of Saddam Hussein. But how could such a thing happen in the United States of America, "the land of the free" and the home of the First Amendment?

Easy. Judge Kent's threats are simply a logical result of the new tolerance, the aggressive ideology that opposes Christianity and shelters idolatry. The new tolerance, because it is based on the view that all truth claims are equal because they are culturally created and conditioned, *must* not only oppose but squelch any proclamation of absolute truth. This explains why the name of Jesus so often invites such strong reactions from otherwise reasonable individuals and groups. As Professor John D. Woodbridge states, "Jesus' claim that he is the way, the truth, and the life makes politically correct moderns gag. It is the ultimate heresy."[2]

Such repression of Christianity is just one of the ominous implications of the new tolerance.

THE DEATH OF TRUTH

America—indeed, almost all of Western culture—was once guided by God's unchanging truth. In the Scriptures, God revealed to mankind that there are certain absolute truths—that is, they are true for all people, in all places, and for all time. Murder and adultery are wrong for all people (Exodus 20:13-14). Stealing and lying are wrong for all people (Leviticus 19:11). Kindness and compassion (Ephesians 4:32) and humility (Philippians 2:1-11) are right for all people.

For several millennia, our laws were established according to God's standards. Our morality was judged according to his requirements. But that is no longer the case. With few exceptions, we now establish our standards and judge morality according to a far more flexible concept of truth, one that suggests that there are no absolutes—that all truth is relative and subjective; right and wrong differ from person to person and from culture to culture.

Such a view is reflected in such oft-heard statements as

- "No one has the right to tell me what's right or wrong!"
- "I can't tell you what's right or wrong; you must decide that for yourself."
- "It's wrong to try to impose your morals on someone else!"
- "I have the right to do whatever I want as long as I'm not hurting anyone."
- "You have to do what you think is right."
- "Those may be the values your parents taught you, but my parents taught me different."
- "Look . . . that's *your* opinion."

The result, of course, is the death of truth. Truth no longer exists as an objective reality in the world of the new tolerance, which means, in turn, that morality is dead as well. As the late author Dr. Francis Schaeffer said,

> If there is no absolute moral standard, then one cannot say in a final sense that anything is right or wrong. By absolute we mean that which always applies [to all people], that which provides a final or ultimate standard. There must be an absolute if there are to be morals, and there must be an absolute if there are to be real values. If there is no absolute beyond man's ideas, then there is no final appeal to

judge between individuals and groups whose moral judgments conflict. We are merely left with conflicting opinions.[3]

And if all that is left are conflicting opinions, well, then, who are you to tell anyone that his or her opinion is wrong? This is precisely what Spanish philosopher Fernando Savater referred to when he said, "All opinions are equal [and] there is no rational way to discern between them."[4]

Thus does the new tolerance insert itself into our minds and into our children's minds, eroding the foundations of truth on which our faith and morality are based. This leaves us all vulnerable to Satan's destructive tricks, branding anyone who dares to stand for objective truth and absolute standards as an intolerant bigot who has no right to speak, a fanatic who must be silenced in order that progress may continue.

THE DISAPPEARANCE OF VIRTUE

- Bravery. Honor. Integrity.
- Reverence. Respect. Civility.
- Humility. Generosity. Compassion.

If you are like most Christians, you want to be known for those kinds of qualities. And, if you are like most Christian parents, pastors, or teachers, you desperately want to instill those qualities in your children, church, or students. But as you look around you, you fear that you won't be able to impart such things as honor and integrity to those who come after you.

Do you know *why* it seems so hard to pass such values on to the next generation these days? Because such concepts are meaningless in a culture dominated by the new tolerance. If all beliefs, lifestyles, and truth claims are equal, how can one exalt humility as a virtue? Who can say that civility is any more right than insolence or that bravery is more commendable than cowardice or that truth is better than a lie?

This is one reason the 1993 riots in South-Central Los Angeles[5] (which victimized many black and Asian shopkeepers and property owners as well as innocent bystanders) did not prompt universal cries of outrage at such lawlessness and destruction but instead brought appeals for tolerant understanding of the rioters' behavior. In an era of the new tolerance, what moral authority can pronounce such random violence as wrong?

As the new tolerance increasingly displaces all other virtues in our schools, government, society, and churches, it will become increasingly difficult to impart biblical, Christian values to succeeding generations.

THE DEMISE OF JUSTICE

Not only does the dawn of new tolerance signal the death of truth, it also sounds the death knell for justice. Like truth, justice used to be a dominant virtue in Western culture. But justice and the new tolerance cannot coexist because they are antithetical to each other.

Don Closson, of Probe Ministries, writes:

> While [advocates of the new tolerance] might refer to justice occasionally, it cannot be the foundation of their movement. This is for the simple reason that justice is not possible without truth. In order for someone to say that actions or words [are unjust], they are assuming that a moral order [apart from one's self] really does exist. Injus-

tice implies that justice exists, justice implies that moral laws exist, and laws imply that a law-giver exists.[6]

In a society dominated by the new tolerance, justice will be increasingly overshadowed by the competing demands of every special-interest group, from environmentalists, human-rights activists, and farmers to gays and lesbians, abortionists, and the gambling industry. The deciding factor in any decision will no longer be a question of justice but simply a question of which group can yell the loudest, lobby the longest, and inspire the most fear and outrage. Court cases will be swayed more and more frequently by public opinion. National leaders will base their decisions on polls rather than law or ethics, aided increasingly by a media that reports public sentiment instead of news.

As a result, justice—the ethic that gave birth and success to the antislavery, women's suffrage, and civil-rights struggles of past generations—will die. The word will still be used, of course, but it will no longer mean that which is just. . . . It will mean that which is most popular or pragmatic.

THE LOSS OF CONVICTION

G. K. Chesterton, the versatile English author who strongly influenced the life and writing of C. S. Lewis, once remarked, "Tolerance is a virtue of a man without convictions." His statement points to another implication of the new tolerance: the loss of conviction.

The dictionary defines *conviction* as "the state of being convinced."[7] But if I sincerely consider everyone's beliefs, lifestyles, and truth claims as *equal* to my own (even when they contradict my beliefs, lifestyles, and truth claims), I can no longer feel any genuine conviction regarding my own beliefs. The new tolerance requires me to admit that I may be as easily mistaken or deluded as my neighbor. If there is no truth that is "more true" than any other "truth," then there is no truth worth defending. If there is no truth worth defending, there is no room for conviction.

This fact was vividly illustrated in a recent U.S. political campaign when the candidate stated that, though he was personally opposed to abortion, he would defend a woman's "right to choose." His position, while politically artful, showed a typically postmodern lack of conviction. And that loss of conviction characterizes not only that particular politician but the entire culture of this radical new tolerance.

The new tolerance is not only making moral zombies of politicians and pundits, it is creating a generation that is both unable and unwilling to defend the Christian faith and live a life defined by Christian convictions.

THE PRIVATIZATION OF FAITH

Stephen L. Carter coined the phrase "the culture of disbelief" to describe the prevailing hostility in Western culture toward public expressions of faith. Jay Sekulow and Keith Fournier, in their book, *And Nothing but the Truth*, describe it as "religious cleansing," an echo of the ethnic cleansing practiced by the Bosnian Serbs in the horrific Bosnian conflict:

> The religious cleansers operate under the guise of civil liberty and the U.S. Constitution, contending in the political arena and the courts that the so-called separation of church and state means that religious beliefs, values, and practices should be barred from the public square.

Religious people can sit in their homes and places of worship and discuss political, moral, and social issues, and they can vote their consciences. But if they move beyond these borders and step into city hall, or the courts, or the public schools, or virtually any community arena, they become trespassers, violators to be hurled back into the private sphere where their ideas cannot affect, or even threaten to affect, anyone but themselves.[8]

In a culture where the new tolerance reigns, you and your children will be increasingly pressured to keep quiet about your faith . . . and to feel inferior because of it. You and your children will be expected to keep "your morality" private. You and your children will be barred from juries and banned from public forums because your opinions, colored as they are by religion, will be considered "prejudiced."[9]

Of course, to be fair, it is not all public expressions of faith that the new tolerance seeks to bar from the public square. Those with no convictions about truth and morality are encouraged to speak up. Those of non-Western faiths are often acclaimed. For example, the Dalai Lama, the spiritual leader of Tibetan Buddhism, who received the Nobel Peace Prize in 1989, has been greeted warmly by top political leaders in every country he has visited, including the United States. And, although Christian studies are off-limits in public universities and colleges, Buddhist studies departments are readily available in many of our institutions of higher learning.[10]

Why the difference? The agenda of the new tolerance is not to privatize (and "ghetto-ize") *all* faiths—only those that proclaim a belief in absolute truth—primarily Christianity and Orthodox Judaism.

THE TYRANNY OF THE INDIVIDUAL

Trouble began to brew as the graduation ceremonies for West High School in Salt Lake City, Utah, approached. The school choir was practicing for the ceremonies. Two of the songs they planned to sing, traditional favorites at the school, contained references to "God" and "Lord."

One student, however, objected to the songs. She claimed that they were "offensive" and "violated her civil rights." So she sued the school, and the Federal Court of Appeals in Denver prohibited the choir from singing the songs at the graduation ceremonies.

That incident illustrates what Chuck Colson has called "the tyranny of the individual—in which one person can obstruct the rights of the majority." Colson goes on to write:

> If the student had been requesting the right not to partici-
> pate, that is something we can all agree upon. She could be
> excused, opt out as Christians often do in sex-education
> classes. But she was demanding something more: that the
> majority be prevented from singing songs she didn't agree
> with.[11]

Under the aegis of the new tolerance, our society has created a new civil right: the right not to be offended, nor even to have to listen to competing truth claims. And, as Colson says further, "A society that isolates itself from competing truth claims will inevitably descend into oppression and tyranny."

In his article "The Politics of Separation," William A. Henry III adds the startling observation that

> [Advocates of the new tolerance] consider a claim of ha-
> rassment essentially unchallengeable, regardless of fact,

61

because the only meaningful perception of grievance is that of the alleged victim.[12]

In other words, the facts or fairness of a situation don't matter; all that matters is whether someone's feelings were hurt. In such a climate, of course, you and your children will be vulnerable to charges of insensitivity, intolerance, and more—such as "religious harassment," for example—if you transgress, knowingly or unknowingly, someone's right not to be offended or challenged.

THE DISINTEGRATION OF HUMAN RIGHTS

Calvin J. Camp, in a letter to *USA Today,* reacted with shock to a news article reporting the signing of a nuclear pact with China. The article indicated that, though the leaders of the two countries had signed the pact, the American president had "sparred" with China's Jiang Zemin over human-rights issues. Camp wrote:

> It seems to be a particularly American trait to look down our noses at other cultures and proclaim ourselves morally superior. . . .
>
> The Chinese approach to human rights is not wrong; it is simply a Chinese approach. Their "mystic chords of memory" are different from ours. They have no memory of a Jefferson or Madison but recall rampaging English and Japanese soldiers. As a result, they cherish stability.
>
> When dissidents threaten this stability, they are dealt with in a Chinese manner. It would be refreshing if our leaders would acknowledge this. . . .[13]

Do you see what that letter writer is saying? In this age of the new tolerance, any advocacy of human rights, particularly on an international basis, is rendered absurd.

When the new tolerance is applied to different cultural values, it is usually identified by the term *multiculturalism*. The basic belief of multiculturalism (as it is widely taught in the public educational system) is that all cultural values, beliefs, lifestyles, and truth claims are equal; there is no standard by which one can judge one cultural value as "better" or "worse" than that which exists in another culture. If truth and morality are cultural creations that cannot be adequately understood (much less communicated) between differing cultures, there are no grounds for any person or nation to protest such abhorrent cultural practices as widow burning (burning living widows on their husbands' funeral pyres) or the forced abortion and infanticide that results from China's severe reproductive laws. If you contend—or even imply—otherwise, then you are being "anti-multicultural," or intolerant.

Indeed, one feminist columnist admitted as much in a widely discussed 1992 editorial on clitoridectomies (the forcible genital mutilation performed on young females in many Islamic countries, in which the clitoris is cut off, often without an anesthetic, to prevent the woman from experiencing sexual pleasure and thus, it is thought, preclude the possibility of sexual promiscuity and adultery). Journalist Andrea Park wrote that, though she despised the oppression of women and wished to condemn the custom, she had no standard by which to judge other cultures:

> How can I argue against a culture I haven't tried to understand? Is it relevant that I, an outsider, may find the prac-

tice cruel? As hard as it is for me to admit, the answer is no.[14]

True to the principles and ideals of the new tolerance, Park's editorial sounded the death knell of human rights. If all beliefs, lifestyles, and truth claims are culturally defined and equally valid, Park and her culture have no right to defend the human rights of those living in other cultures. Nor do you or your children.

THE DOMINANCE OF FEELING

Another implication of the new tolerance is that feelings have begun to replace fact in human deliberations and decisions; emotion has displaced reason, and style is winning out over substance. Ryszard Legutko, in his essay, "The Trouble with Toleration," writes:

> We are witnessing today the decline of strong philosophy, inhumanely objective and hierarchical, and the triumph of essentially weak rhetoric: the criteria of social coexistence, adaptable and malleable, have begun to play a more important role than the suprahuman criteria of truth.[15]

What is he saying? That feelings have become more important than fact, a situation illustrated by the common practice of substituting the term "I *feel*" for "I *think*" in phrases like "I feel that our schools are doing a good job," and "I feel what a person does in the privacy of his own home is nobody's business but his own."

Duke University political scientist James David Barber puts it this way:

I think a lot of "impressionism"—a detestation of reason in favor of emotion—is happening now.[16]

As feelings rule in place of ideas in our society, men and women will increasingly believe nonsense ("If I *feel* it, how can it be wrong?") and dissent will be disallowed ("How can you disagree with how I *feel?*").

THE EXALTATION OF NATURE

The twentieth-century German philosopher Martin Heidegger challenged the notion that mankind enjoyed a special status over nature; he argued that human beings are no different from any other object or being in nature.

Heidegger's views have come to fruition in today's atmosphere of new tolerance, as Gene Edward Veith points out in his book *Postmodern Times:*

Whereas modernism sought human control over nature, postmodernism exalts nature at the expense of human beings. While a love of nature and a concern for the environment are laudable, many environmentalists go to anti-human extremes. David Brown, former head of the Sierra Club, sees the destruction of human life as being no more tragic than the destruction of the wilderness. "While the death of young men in war is unfortunate," he says, "it is no more serious than [the] touching of mountains and wilderness areas by humankind." The Finnish Green Party activist Pentti Linkola . . . goes so far as to say that he has more sympathy for threatened insect species than for children dying of hunger in Africa.[17]

Environmental extremism has also spawned the Animal Rights movement. *In a world without absolutes, there is no basis for saying that human beings are any better than any other species*. . . . According to Ingrid Newkirk, president of People for the Ethical Treatment of Animals, "A rat is a pig is a dog is a boy."[18] Her point is that a human child is not innately better and should have no higher privileges than a dog, a pig, or a rat. [italics added][19]

In a world and an era in which "all is equal," human beings—even children—should not expect any more consideration than animals, forests, or insects. In fact, they may often receive less.

THE DESCENT INTO EXTREMES

A seventeen-year-old Canadian girl named Onis Cartier decided one day recently to walk her dog along a downtown street in Ottawa. Her husband, Cory, accompanied her. Nothing unusual about that—except that she was wearing no clothing from the waist up. After nearly causing a series of traffic accidents, Onis explained that she had decided not to wait for the city council vote regarding the issue of women going topless in public.

"I decided to do it because I finally had the guts," said Onis. "I'm just showing every other female they can do it, so why don't they, too?"

And she's right—legally, at least. As a result of an Ontario Court of Appeal ruling, it has been legal in Canada for women to bare their breasts in public since December 1996. The pending city-council vote Onis cited concerned a woman's right to go "topless in municipal swimming pools and public beaches." The earlier court of appeal ruling came as a result of an indecency conviction against another Canadian woman, Gwen Jacobs, who received a fine for taking a topless stroll in July 1991. The court of appeal overturned her conviction.[20]

Unthinkable? Maybe yesterday, but not today. It is simply another implication of the new tolerance. If all beliefs, behaviors, lifestyles, and truth claims must be tolerated as equally valid, then even the most outrageous and extreme claims must be granted the same treatment as all others. This descent into extremes is vividly illustrated in the recent statement of the Utah chapter of the National Organization of Women (NOW) proposing polygamy as a solution for the problems of working mothers.

"It seems like a pretty good idea for professional women, who can proceed with their careers and have someone at home they can trust to watch their kids. It solves the daycare problem," stated Lucy Mallon, Vice Chairman of Utah NOW. Ellen George, State Secretary for Utah NOW, added, "This isn't blatant support for polygamy, but maybe it can work for some people, and maybe it can make raising children easier for those trying to juggle careers and motherhood."[21]

Alan Keyes, former ambassador to the United Nations, said in reference to the NOW statement on polygamy, "I knew this was going to happen. . . . If [we] accept the liberal position on gay marriage . . . then there is no argument, no grounds, for standing against polygamy. [We] have given the game away. . . . We are witnessing it here in our time."[22]

We are, indeed. Consider the case of two young boys, ages five and eight, who were caught in the middle of an ugly custody battle. Their mother, a Christian, found herself in the midst of divorce when her husband expressed his desire to undergo a "gender reassignment." In other words, he wanted to have surgery so that he could become a "woman" and live with another woman as a practicing "lesbian." He also sought custody of the boys. By the time of the custody proceedings, the father had already undergone the surgery and was living in a relationship with another male who had experienced the same surgery, as well as a third male who "only dressed as a woman" (the threesome did not last, however, and the father thereafter married his "lesbian" partner).

The Alliance Defense Fund, hearing of the case, came to the mother's aid and was able to prevent the father and his partner(s) from gaining custody of the boys, but not until the case was taken before the state court of appeals, *which reversed the lower court's decision to rule in the father's favor!*[23]

Can things get any more bizarre? you may wonder. Unfortunately, they can ... and they will, if the progress of the new tolerance continues unchecked.

Tragically, these are just a few of the implications of the new tolerance. As this dangerous movement continues to grow, it will place you, your children, and your church at the middle of a swirling cultural storm that could rip the foundations of faith and morality out from under you and leave you and those you love with nowhere to stand.

But there are steps that can be taken to stem the tide of this new tolerance. In fact, I believe it's even possible to *turn the tide* and "overcome evil with good" (Romans 12:21). But in order to do that, we first must understand the tactics of the new tolerance.

Chapter 5

THE TACTICS OF
TOLERANCE

George Orwell, an English author whose real name was Eric Blair, painted a grim picture of human society's future in his famous book, *1984*. The book depicted life in totalitarian England (called Airstrip One in the book) ruled by Big Brother, a ubiquitous leader who is never seen but hears all and sees all. Orwell's totalitarian society was characterized by "Newspeak" and "Doublethink."

Newspeak was a language that replaced many words with new, politically acceptable terms: the Ministry of Peace ran the ongoing war between the world's three surviving superstates, the Ministry of Love administered the secret police's campaign of oppression, the Ministry of Plenty dealt in scarcities, and the Ministry of Truth disseminated propaganda and revised history. *Doublethink* was a term Orwell used to describe Big Brother's equation of contradictory ideas: "War is Peace, Freedom is Slavery, Ignorance is Strength."

Perhaps the most memorable feature of Orwell's vision, however, was the terrible consequences that would follow what the society called "thought crimes," any failure or refusal to think acceptable thoughts or to speak approved words. People who were guilty of thought crimes were censured, ridiculed, tortured, and silenced . . . by death, if necessary.

Happily, the year 1984 came and went, and Orwell's vision remained unfulfilled. The world's governments did not coalesce into three warring superstates. England was not absorbed by totalitarian Oceania. Two-way "telescreens" were not installed in every home to broadcast propaganda and spy on people's private lives.

But other features of *1984* have seen fulfillment. They have not been brought about by a centralized totalitarian government, however; they have been spread through our culture and society and into our churches and homes as the result of a philosophy—namely, postmodernism and the new tolerance.

We are not suggesting that this is some kind of human conspiracy, a worldwide plot carried out among government officials, financial moguls, media personnel, and educators. Oh, there may be some who are aware of the destructive influence of the new tolerance and propagate it intentionally and maliciously. But the vast majority of those who spread the Newspeak and Doublethink of the new tolerance—lawmakers and policy makers, news reporters, educators, and cause supporters—do so unconsciously, along with the unsuspecting homemaker, the scout leader, the bus driver, and the used-car salesman. For the concept itself is fast becoming "institutionalized," accepted by the vast majority through constant exposure and influence. But notice the key word: *unsuspecting.* Generally speaking, many who are spreading the new tolerance are sincere people trying to grapple with the death of objective, knowable truth in modern society (as described in chapter 3); they have been duped, and they are totally unaware of it because *the deceived do not know they have been deceived.* They are oblivious to the fact that they are victims of a dangerous philosophy.

But though the spread of the new tolerance is not a human

conspiracy, there is a grand conspirator working behind the scenes, a chessmaster moving the pawns to his advantage. He is, of course, our adversary, "the god of this age"[1] and "the father of lies."[2] He knows the truth of God's Word and the power of the gospel,[3] and so he has worked, by degrees, to undermine the Christian faith, impede its spread, and raise the idols of post-modernism. And, as we shall see, the tactics of tolerance are as diabolical as anything Orwell imagined.

DOUBLETHINK AND THE NEW TOLERANCE

Remember the fantasy world of Alice in *Through the Looking Glass* and *Alice in Wonderland*? One aspect of that "wonder-land" is similar to the world of the new tolerance.

> "Now I'll give *you* something to believe," said the Queen. "I'm just one hundred and one, five months and a day."
>
> "I ca'n't believe *that!*" said Alice.
>
> "Ca'n't you?" the Queen said in a pitying tone. "Try again: draw a long breath and shut your eyes."
>
> Alice laughed. "There's no use trying," she said: "one *ca'n't* believe impossible things."
>
> "I daresay you haven't had much practice," said the Queen. "When I was your age, I always did it for half-an-hour a day. Why, sometimes, I've believed as many as six impossible things before breakfast."

One of the most basic tactics of tolerance is the insistence that it is possible to believe impossibilities, a tactic eerily remi-niscent of Orwell's *1984,* in which the protagonist, George Win-ston, was tortured until he swore that two plus two equals five . . . and believed it! Today's tolerance performs a similar feat in the minds of young and old, painting such "impossibility think-ing" as very modern and intellectual.

For example, Hinduism teaches that when a soul dies it be-comes reincarnated in another form; Islam (among others) as-serts that souls spend eternity in heaven or hell. Now, basic logic—the law of noncontradiction—insists that two contra-dictory ideas cannot both be true. But the new tolerance is grounded in postmodern thought, which asserts, among other things, that logic and linear thought are Western and therefore oppressive. So it is not only possible, *it is necessary* to believe two (or more) contradictory things at once.

Therefore, in the world of the new tolerance, all ideas about what happens to the soul when it dies *are equally true.* As are all religions, all "sexual orientations," all values, and all beliefs . . . even though they may be contradictory. (The exceptions, of course, are any religions, values, beliefs, etc., that proclaim the existence of objective truth).

That kind of doublethink works well for the proponents of the new tolerance because it turns the Temple of Tolerance into a virtual mall of idolatrous beliefs and behaviors . . . and makes it all the more tempting to your children, and perhaps even to you.

NEWSPEAK AND THE NEW TOLERANCE

The proponents of the new tolerance appear to have borrowed the concept of Newspeak from Orwell's book, as well. As we dis-cussed in chapter 2, a fundamental premise of the new tolerance is characteristic of this Newspeak: it falsely equates the *person* with the person's *attitudes and actions;* it says that not only are all human beings created equal but all beliefs, behaviors, lifestyles, and truth claims are equal. As a result, the word *tolerance* is given a new definition, to mean not only accepting a *person* who differs from you but also agreeing with, approving, and even participating in that person's beliefs, behaviors, and lifestyle.

Drawing such false equations is one of the primary tactics of the new tolerance.

Nonagreement Is Phobia

One of the Orwellian tactics of the new tolerance is the negative labeling of any disagreement or objection as "phobic."

Debra J. Saunders, writing in *The San Francisco Chronicle,* reported the reaction of one "old-fashioned" father who protested the content of the sex education his son was receiving in public school.

"When I complained that my elementary school son was too young to understand homosexuality," the father said, "they called me a 'homophobe.' [They] wouldn't listen, they just called me names."[4]

The treatment that father received reveals a key tactic of the new tolerance. Unfortunately, if you, your children, or your church register any disagreement with or objection to the agenda of the new tolerance, the result will likely be labeling and name-calling . . . by the very people who claim to value tolerance.

Nonconformity Is Hate

Dr. Jim Aist, professor of plant pathology at Cornell University in Ithaca, New York, was "accused of sexual harassment, discrimination, and abuse of power. Students staged a six-hour sit-in in protest against him. His own chairman and dean pursued charges against him. He was made to answer charges without being allowed to know what they were. He endured the scrutiny of ten investigations in two years. He had to stand by as the press paraded accusations against him."[5]

What was Dr. Aist's crime? He had posted flyers on campus offering "Help to Homosexuals." The flyers offered—free to students and faculty—carefully researched scientific information about the cause of homosexuality and guidance for homosexuals who wished to leave the homosexual lifestyle.

Gay activists complained, however, that "Aist's posters and encouragement to lesbian, gay, bisexual and transgender students to repent and go 'straight' viciously aggravate the self-hatred and depression that [gay] people are forced to feel." The group DASH (Direct Action to Stop Homophobia) accused Aist of "creating a hostile . . . environment" and of encouraging violence against homosexuals (interestingly, not one student or faculty member requested the packet of research; the animosity that was aimed at Dr. Aist was based not on the substance of his research but on the emotionalism his opponents managed to create).

When Campus Crusade for Christ launched a similar poster and ad campaign called "Every Student's Choice," telling of homosexuals who had found acceptance in the church and deliverance from the homosexual lifestyle, several newspapers refused to accept the ads and a University of Virginia group posted a flyer comparing Campus Crusade for Christ with the KKK and bearing the slogan "Cruelty, Hate and Dishonesty are not Christian Values!"

This tactic of labeling any opposing view with words like *hostility, hatred, cruelty,* and *bigotry* has repeatedly proven effective for the proponents of the new tolerance.

Conviction Is Fanaticism

One of the necessary results of the new tolerance is the loss of convictions (see chapter 4). If no "truth" is any more true than any other "truth," then there is no truth worth defending. If there is no truth worth defending, there is no room for conviction—particularly religious conviction (and, even more particularly, Christian conviction).

As a result, those who have been deceived by the new tolerance naturally view a person of conviction with suspicion or contempt. Debra J. Saunders, a columnist for *The San Francisco Chronicle*, quoted one mother's comments about her children's public-school experiences: "My children's teachers say they want students to think for themselves, but when my children say they think they should obey their parents or God, they're ridiculed. What kind of diversity can you have when children are pressured into thinking the same things?"[6]

But that kind of reaction to religious conviction is the only possible result of a philosophical system that contends that all truth claims are equal . . . except truth claims that say all truth claims are *not* equal!

In today's climate of new tolerance, if you and your loved ones display strong Christian convictions, your convictions will expose you as fanatics, whether you feel like fanatics or not. Because, in the Newspeak of the new tolerance, convictions are fanatical, inasmuch as convictions imply the superiority of one idea (that which is held with conviction) over all others, which is in direct opposition to the "all is equal" doctrine of new tolerance.

Christian Creeds/Prayers/Symbols Are Discriminatory

Another key tenet of the new tolerance Newspeak is the designation of Christian creeds, prayers, symbols, and similar expressions of faith as discriminatory.

For example, the local chapter of InterVarsity Christian Fellowship on the Carleton (Ottawa) University campus was expelled from the school's student union, making it ineligible for funding, access to facilities, etc. The reason? IVCF's requirement that club members sign the InterVarsity statement of faith. The student union claimed that such a requirement violated a policy allowing equal access to all clubs. In other words, it is discrimination for a *Christian* club to expect its members to assent to a Christian creed.[7]

Or consider the case of Bishop Knox, a school principal in Jackson, Mississippi. The student body at Knox's school had voted to have a prayer read over the school intercom each morning. Knox allowed the following non-sectarian prayer to be read: "Almighty God, we ask that You bless our parents, teachers, and country throughout the day." When word of this morning exercise leaked out, the ACLU protested vehemently. Knox was dismissed.[8] And, of course, there are frequent instances of community Christmas trees, manger scenes, and other Christian symbols being banned, such as the case one December in which parents of public-school students were asked to "come to school and share with the class about Kwanzaa, the religious holiday practices of their Buddhist faith and Muslim faith as well as the traditions and practices of Hanukkah." When one parent attempted to share the true meaning of Christmas, using a Nativity scene as a visual aid, the presentation was prohibited.[9]

In a society dominated by the doctrine of the new tolerance, any recognition of or reference to Christian creeds, prayers, or symbols (or those even remotely so) is seen as an attempt by the "dominant" culture (Christianity, in this case) to discriminate against other cultures and faiths. Never mind, of course, that we now live in a day and age in which Christianity is often victimized by "the one bigotry that seems to be acceptable these days—bigotry against . . . Christians," according to one commentator.[10] Such bigotry against Christians and the Christian faith is not only acceptable but even laudable because in the Newspeak of the new tolerance, Christian creeds, prayers, and symbols are a dangerous form of discrimination, since they each proclaim the unique claims of Jesus.

Selective Segregation Is Justice

In the 1950s and 1960s, the civil-rights movement in the United States waged a war against segregation. At that time, many public restaurants, restrooms, schools—even drinking fountains—were designated for use by "Whites only." Oklahoma required separate telephone booths for "Whites" and "Negroes." Arkansas designated separate gambling tables. Many courts kept separate Bibles for swearing in witnesses. As a result of the civil-rights movement, such reprehensible practices were abolished.

Similar campaigns also fought segregation by caste in India and dismantled the apartheid that existed in South Africa until the early 1990s. But ironically, one of the results of the new tolerance is a new wave of segregation and division along ethnic and cultural lines.

For example, the University of Pennsylvania recently

funded a "Black" yearbook, "even though only 6% of the student body is black and all other groups appeared in the general yearbook. Vassar, Dartmouth, and the University of Illinois have allowed separate graduation activities and ceremonies for minority students. California State University at Sacramento has established an official 'college within a college' for blacks."[11] And the International Black Buyers and Manufacturers Expo and Conference, "an association representing more than 1,000 black-owned businesses," recently informed large American firms like Hallmark Cards and Giant Food that products related to Kwanzaa (the late-December celebration of African heritage) should be produced and sold only by Blacks.[12]

A similar incident occurred when Welshman Jonathan Pryce and Filipino Lea Salonga were cast to play the leads in the musical *Miss Saigon* on Broadway. "Asian actors protested a white actor playing the role of a sleazy Vietnamese pimp trying to emigrate to the United States."[13] By the end of the year, the producers awarded the role to someone with the appropriate racial qualifications: Filipino-Chinese actor Francis Ruivivar.

Perhaps the most dramatic example of the "selective segregation is justice" equation is occurring in Quebec, Canada, where the drive to politically segregate French Quebec from the rest of the nation has gained increasing momentum. Charles Krauthammer says:

> The bitterness of French Canada's drive to amputate its
> century-old confederation with English Canada tells us
> much about our unexamined belief in the strength and
> beauty of multiculturalism. . . . They are a living refutation
> of the warm and cozy notion, based more on hope than
> on history, of multicultural harmony and strength. . . .

One looks at Canada and wonders whether the current naive and confident American celebration of cultural diversity—with its insistence on group rights over individual rights, sectarian history over American history, ethnic culture over a common culture—is leading us down a path from which there is no escape.[14]

In the world of the new tolerance, selective discrimination and segregation are not only legitimate but laudable . . . *if* the discrimination or segregation favors a "minority" group over the so-called dominant culture. In the U.S. and Canada, of course, this "dominant culture" is alternately identified as white, male, English-speaking, and Christian. Of course, who gets to define which cultures are dominant is unclear, and whether such dominance can be shown objectively is never considered because in the postmodern view, *truth* does not exist; only the power to win the argument or promote one's own ideology matters.[15]

By drawing such false equations, the new tolerance creates a new lexicon for society that elevates postmodern ideals and suppresses the Christian ideals of righteousness, conviction, freedom, and justice for all. And, in so doing, it threatens your rights and your faith, as well as those of your children and your church.

THOUGHT CRIMES AND THE NEW TOLERANCE

In the Oceania of Orwell's creation, disagreement and dissent were labeled "thought crimes" and were severely punished. The era of the new tolerance has ushered in an eerily Orwellian approach to disagreement. For instance, over the past three decades, I have addressed millions of high school and college students about Jesus Christ and the historical evidence for his life and resurrection. When I began touring and lecturing, I would often get heckled. I even welcomed it at times because the hecklers would respond to the substance of my message, saying such things as, "Prove it!" and, "I don't believe you," thus giving me the opportunity to support my statements with evidence.

In the past few years, however, I have witnessed a startling shift. Now, rather than responding to the substance of my message, my detractors invariably say things like, "How dare you say that?" "You're intolerant!" "Who do you think you are that you have the corner on truth?" and, "What right do you have to make a moral judgment on someone else's lifestyle?" The issue is no longer the truth of the message but the right to proclaim it . . . because any message that challenges the new tolerance—either explicitly or implicitly—constitutes a "thought crime"!

And, just as in Orwell's vision, one of the tactics of the new tolerance is to respond to such thought crimes with punishment and persecution. For example, in January 1994, the Supreme Court of the United States ruled that a 1970 federal racketeering law (the Racketeer Influenced and Corrupt Organizations Act, known as RICO) applied not only to organized crime but also to abortion-protest groups such as Operation Rescue. RICO has not been applied so vigorously—if at all—to other protestors such as labor groups, animal-rights organizations, environmentalists, or homosexual activists. As Frank Jamison, professor of law at the University of Denver and a former Colorado County judge, commented, "If I were an abortion protestor and had a little to protect, like my house, I might think twice" before joining Operation Rescue.[16] Abortion protestors seem to hold a special status due, perhaps, to their "politically incorrect" views.

Forest M. Mims III, an accomplished freelance writer, was apparently guilty of thought crimes, too. Mims had received an offer from the editor of *Scientific American* to be the new author of the magazine's "The Amateur Scientist" column. When the magazine flew him to New York for a formal interview, the editor noticed several Christian magazines on Mim's writing résumé.

"He stopped me there," recalls Mims, who is a deacon and Sunday school teacher at First Baptist Church of Segum, Texas. "He said, 'Do you accept the Darwinian theory of evolution?' I said 'no,' and the rest of the meeting went downhill very rapidly." After that, Mims was amazed at the turn the questioning took. He was also asked, "Are you a fundamentalist Christian?" and "Do you believe in the sanctity of life?"[17]

Mims was guilty, all right. His crime? Holding the "wrong" beliefs. And not holding the "right" ones. For such thought crimes, the *Scientific American* sent Mims packing, rejecting him as the author of the magazine's most popular column. After all, some things just can't be tolerated.

The strategies and tactics of the new tolerance—encouraging "Doublethink," employing "Newspeak," and eradicating "thought crimes"—are not only reminiscent of Orwell's *1984;* they also pose a clear and present danger to anyone—you and your family included—who does not bow to the teachings of postmodernism.

Responding to questions about his experience with *Scientific American,* Mims warned, "I've tried to turn the other cheek for now, but at some point I've got to . . . put a halt to this kind of discrimination before it gets too advanced. If Christians don't act now, it may be you who doesn't get a job next time."[18]

It is time for Christians to respond. If we do not, our freedoms will be increasingly eroded and our children's faith will be increasingly undermined, our culture will crumble all around us, and our churches will be destroyed from within.

But for that response to be effective in defusing the new tolerance and preserving the faith for us and our children, we need to do more than simply defend our civil and religious rights. We need much more than that. We need far better than that. We need a strategy, a plan. We need a positive response that will not only defend but also advance the kingdom of heaven.

Chapter 6

THE MORE
EXCELLENT WAY

I've seen the skit performed many times at youth retreats and church camps. An unsuspecting actor is drafted into the starring role and given instructions. When the time for the skit comes, the actor enters, crawling slowly across the floor of the stage or meeting room, gasping and panting, "Water! Water!" The actor's tongue lolls from his mouth, and he repeats, in a rasping voice, "Water! Water!" He drags himself a few more feet and then repeats his dramatic line: "Water! Water!"

Finally, a fellow cast member appears onstage and, in a move that surprises both actor and audience, throws a bucket of water in the poor actor's face.

It is a hilarious moment, of course, if a little bit cruel.

But why is the skit's climax so shocking and funny? Because the actor's pleas receive an unexpected and, to a thirsty man or woman crawling across a desert, ineffective response. The plea for "Water! Water!" was a desperate cry for a *drink*. But the response, while it may be momentarily refreshing to both giver and receiver, does no good.

Similarly, Christians have typically responded to the new

tolerance in ways that, while they may have been momentarily satisfying, have proven woefully inadequate. Our responses have ranged from capitulation: attempting "to mend [our] ways, to bend [our] beliefs to modernity in order to make them more acceptable"[1]—to conflict: attempting to win back by political means the Christian consensus that has been lost in Western countries and cultures. But neither of these extremes—nor the middle ground of compromise between them—is appropriate or effective.

So, if capitulation, compromise, and conflict are not the answer, what *is?* How *do* we counter a cultural movement that threatens to undermine our children's faith and erode their convictions of right and wrong? How *do* we maintain a Daniel-like stand for truth and righteousness in the face of ridicule, even persecution? What is an effective Christian response to a culture steeped in the postmodern doctrine of new tolerance?

An Asian Jew who faced an anti-Christian culture that persecuted and eventually killed him once said, there is a "more excellent way" (1 Corinthians 12:31, NASB). It is the way of love.

THE LOOK OF LOVE

"Oh, brother," you might be tempted to respond. "Is that the best you can do?"

It may sound simplistic. After all, the new tolerance is a complex doctrine, a pervasive movement. And it has brought about a culture that is fiercely antagonistic to Christians and to the Christian faith. This is no time to whistle a happy little rendition of "All We Need Is Love."

But what I am suggesting is far from simplistic because the

kind of love I am talking about is far from the syrupy counterfeit of love that exists in the popular conception. In fact, I believe that the reason the new tolerance has gained ascendancy in our culture—and the reason the church's response has hitherto been so ineffective—is because we have failed to understand what love really looks like. The image of real, Christian love has grown fuzzy and unfocused in our minds and in the minds of the world. As a result, if we ever hope to respond effectively to the new tolerance, we must recapture *what Christian love looks like*—what it is, what it does, and what it does not do.

I have delivered a talk called "Love Makes It Right" to many thousands of youth and adults around the world. During the talk I typically appeal to the audience, asking if anyone can give me a concise definition of *love*. Some have tried, but I've never had one person offer a clear, satisfying definition of what love is.

On one occasion, I asked a crowd of four thousand Christians to write the definition of *love* on three-by-five-inch index cards, which were later collected. Out of four thousand, only *seven people* managed a biblically consistent definition of *love*.

Here's the point: If we don't know what love really is, *how can we* do *it?*

Oh, we think we know what love is. We know we're supposed to love God and others. *But what does it look like? What does it do?* How does Christian love act in a culture dominated by the new tolerance? Does it mean ignoring the differing beliefs, values, and lifestyles of other people? Does it mean agreeing with them and approving of what they do? Does it mean participating in things God has called sinful?

I believe the answers to these questions lie in several familiar passages of the Bible. Our problem, our lack of success in preventing and responding to the new tolerance has not been because Christian love does not address our modern situation; it has been because we have not fully understood what love is. And because we don't know what love really is, we are unable to "do it."

Love as Christ Loved You

The apostle Paul, the Asian Jew I mentioned earlier, commanded Christians:

> *Be imitators of God, therefore, as dearly loved children and live a life of love, just as Christ loved us. (Ephesians 5:1-2)*

Paul commands us to "love, just as Christ loved us." Why? Because Jesus is the incarnation of God, who is love (1 John 4:8). If you want to know what real love is, take a long, hard look at Jesus.

This is crucial for those of us living in the age of new tolerance because, as we pointed out earlier, the new tolerance equates "who I am" with "what I do" and goes on to assume that any disagreement with or criticism of *what a person does* is intolerance of *the person himself or herself.* The new tolerance says, therefore, that loving acceptance means approval of—even participation in—that person's beliefs, behavior, lifestyle, and truth claims.

But that is not at all how Christ loved. He did not ignore the erroneous beliefs of others; he said to the Pharisees, "You are in error because you do not know the Scriptures or the power of God."[2] He did not agree with or approve of sinful behavior; he told the woman caught in adultery, "Go now and leave your life of sin."[3] He did not participate in activities he disagreed with; the Bible says he was "tempted in every way, just as we are—yet was without sin."[4] But he loved us "while we were still sinners"[5]—and "gave himself up for us."[6]

That is what it means to love as Christ loved us. It means, first of all, recognizing that it is not only possible, it is *essential* to distinguish between who a person is and what a person does. A human being is more—infinitely more—than simply the product of his culture or the sum of his beliefs and behaviors. In order to love as Christ loved us, we must recognize and remember and relate to each person as

1. A human being created in the image of God. Max Lucado, in his book *In the Grip of Grace,* writes:

> One of the finest gifts I ever received is a football signed by thirty former professional quarterbacks. There is nothing unique about this ball. For all I know it was bought at a discount sports store. What makes it unique is the signatures.
>
> The same is true with us. In the scheme of nature *Homo sapiens* are not unique. We aren't the only creatures with flesh and hair and blood and hearts. What makes us special is not our body but the signature of God on our lives. We are his works of art. We are created in his image to do good deeds. We are significant, not because of what we do, but because of whose we are.[7]

Every human being in the world—butcher, baker, candlestick maker, African, American, European, Asian, male, female, young, old, Hindu, Muslim, Catholic, Protestant, murderer or rapist, minister or choir member, rich man, poor man, beggar man, thief—is an infinitely valuable work of art, bearing the signature of God himself.

2. A person for whom Christ died. Many years ago, Bob,

the coauthor of this book, attended a "box-lunch auction" as a teenager. The young women in the group had each made a box lunch for two, and only the auctioneer knew which woman had made which lunch. The young men were allowed to bid on the boxes, and then they would share the lunch with the woman who had made it.

Through some careful investigation, Bob managed to find out which lunch belonged to the young woman he was dating (who later became his wife). Several of his friends, however, watched him carefully and, when he began to bid on that particular lunch, gave him a run for his money! They reasoned (accurately, it turned out) that Bob would know which box lunch his girlfriend had made, and anyone who outbid him would get to have lunch with the beautiful young woman who had made it! They knew the true value of that box lunch because Bob let them see how much he valued it.

Similarly, we can know the true value of our fellow human beings by looking at how much God values them. God showed his great love for every one of us by sending Christ to redeem us with his life (Romans 5:8). This loving act ought to inspire an outpouring of love and respect and acceptance in us toward our fellow human beings. We know the true value of every man, woman, and child among us—regardless of their faults or foibles, their beliefs or behaviors, their sins or shortcomings—because God let us see how much he values them by sending his only Son to die a cruel death to save them.

To love others as Christ loved us means to recognize their infinite and intrinsic value as human beings *altogether apart from their beliefs, behavior, lifestyle, or truth claims.* Whether a person lives a life of virtue or vice, he or she is nonetheless made in the image of God, a priceless soul for whom Christ died.

Whatever they look like, whatever they believe, whatever they do, whatever their lifestyle may be, every human being is of immeasurable worth. And if we love as Christ has loved us, we will accept and respect others on that basis.

But that is not all we must do in order to recapture what Christian love looks like.

Love Your Neighbor as Yourself

An expert in religious law once asked Jesus, "Which is the most important commandment in the law of Moses?"

Jesus replied, " 'You must love the Lord your God with all your heart, all your soul, and all your mind.' This is the first and greatest commandment" (Matthew 22:36-38, NLT).

The first commandment Jesus quoted appears in the sixth chapter of Deuteronomy. Moses declared to all the people, "Hear, O Israel! The Lord is our God, the Lord is one! And you shall love the Lord your God with all your heart and with all your soul and with all your might" (Deuteronomy 6:4-5, NASB). Jesus was declaring that putting God first as the only one true God in our lives and loving him completely was the greatest commandment.

Twentieth-century Christians have done a fair job of preaching that message to the culture of new tolerance. "Hear, O culture of new tolerance! The Lord is our God," we proudly proclaim. "The Lord is the one and only absolute truth!" If only our relativistic culture would hear our proclamation and acknowledge the one true God!

But notice that Jesus didn't stop there. His answer to the religious leaders was not yet complete. After he quoted Deuteronomy 6:4-5, he said, "A second is equally important: 'Love your neighbor as yourself.' All the other commandments and all the demands of the prophets are based on these two commandments" (Matthew 22:39-40, NLT). It is just here that we Christians have misunderstood what real love is and thus failed to respond adequately to the challenge of the new tolerance. But it is also here that we can find the power to diffuse the new tolerance and make a Christlike mark on this culture.

What does it mean to love your neighbor as yourself? We might answer, "Put others first," or, "Treat others the way you want to be treated." And I'm sure it includes that. However, it means much more. I have found that the following concise definition of Christlike love has helped me understand how to love others as I love myself: In very basic terms, *Christian love is making the health, happiness, and spiritual growth of another person as important to you as your own.*

The apostle Paul's words in the book of Ephesians offer further insight into how this definition of Christlike love is lived out. In fact, what I have been saying in this chapter is a reflection of Paul's words in Ephesians 5.

First, Paul instructed husbands, "Love your wives, just as Christ loved the church and gave himself up for her" (v. 25). He defined real love as being *just as Christ loved,* a sacrificial love, a love that valued the church so much that he died for it.

Then Paul went on to say, "Husbands ought to love their wives as their own bodies. He who loves his wife loves himself" (v. 28). That is the great commandment love Jesus talked about in Matthew 22, applied specifically to the marriage relationship. But the next verse explains what it means to live out Christ's command to love another as you love yourself: "For no one ever hated his own flesh, but *nourishes* and *cherishes* it, just as Christ also does the church" (v. 29, NASB, italics added).

To love, then, means to nourish and cherish. But what does *that* mean?

Well, to nourish means to bring to maturity. It means to care for and contribute to the health and vitality of the whole person: mentally, physically, spiritually, and relationally. In other words, if you love someone as you love yourself, you'll nourish that person; you'll help him or her grow "in wisdom and stature, and in favor with God and men" (Luke 2:52). For that reason, to love another person means to try *to provide* whatever is necessary to achieve his or her happiness, health, and spiritual growth.

To *cherish*—the other word Paul uses to describe what it means to love another as you love yourself—does not mean to "adore" or "admire" someone; it means, literally, to protect from the elements. Imagine a nest of newborn eaglets high on a mountain crag, exposed to the sky. An angry thunderstorm is rolling in. The mother eagle swoops down to the nest and spreads her wings over her offspring to protect them from the pounding rain and swirling wind. That's a picture of what it means to cherish someone; it means *to protect* that person from harm, whether physical, spiritual, or emotional.

Most of us are pretty highly motivated to nourish (provide for) and cherish (protect) ourselves. We bundle up when we're cold and fan ourselves when we're hot. We duck to avoid an opponent's blows and swerve to elude an oncoming car. We feed our bodies and enrich our minds. We call the dentist when a toothache throbs and reach for the medicine cabinet when a headache hits. Some of us even fasten our seat belts to prevent physical injury on the highway and monitor our fat and calorie intake to keep ourselves healthy. In short, we generally guard ourselves against harmful things and try to provide constructive and enjoyable things for ourselves. But Ephesians 5:28-29 suggests that Christian love means seeking for another person what we strive to attain ourselves. Christian love actively seeks to promote the good of another person (1 Corinthians 13:6-7); it will attempt to provide for and protect the welfare of that person.

That correct concept of real Christlike love reveals what was wrong with Jim's attitude in his discussion with Chuck back in chapter 2.

"Live and let live," Jim said, when discussing the homosexual lifestyle. But that comment expresses indifference, not love. Would a loving husband sit idly by while his wife choked on a piece of food at the dinner table? Would a loving mother let her child place a hand on a hot stove? Would a loving friend stand safely on the shore while a buddy drowned in a lake?

No, of course not. Because that would not be loving. If we truly love someone, we will strive to protect and provide for that person as we would for ourselves. Thus, Christian love necessarily includes concern about sinful beliefs, behaviors, and lifestyles because, as Max Lucado has written, "disobedience [of God] always results in self-destruction."[8] Christlike love does not just "hate the sin, but love the sinner"; it seeks to prevent the suffering and pain that inevitably accompany disobedience.

So, true compassionate love that seeks to provide for and protect another person's health, happiness, and spiritual growth could not comply with the cultural call: "If you love me, you'll endorse my behavior." Because real love—true love—grieves over the inevitable results of wrong behavior.

LOVE ON THE ROCKS

The new tolerance is erroneously portrayed in today's culture as the most loving way to live. It is associated in people's minds with such things as kindness, peace, cooperation, understanding, even love. To validate someone else's behavior or beliefs is depicted and seen as the loving thing to do.

But such "tolerance" is far from loving. And I am convinced that Christians not only need a renewed vision of what love really looks like, what love does; we also need to grasp clearly what love *does not do*.

Love Won't Ignore the Truth

Jesus once paused by a public well on the long journey from Galilee to Judea, while his disciples trudged into the nearby town to buy a few groceries.

While Jesus sat by the well, a woman approached . . . a Samaritan woman. Not only was it considered scandalous for a Jewish man to speak to a woman—other than a wife or close relative—in public, but the Jews shunned Samaritans. Nonetheless, Jesus spoke to the woman, a doubly loving act on his part.

Notice, however, that he did not ignore the truth of her situation but spoke lovingly *and* straightforwardly to her, addressing her lifestyle not as an "alternate lifestyle" but as a sinful lifestyle that was destructive to her health, happiness, and spiritual well-being:

> He told her, *"Go, call your husband and come back."*
> *"I have no husband,"* she replied.
> *Jesus said to her, "You are right when you say you have no husband. The fact is, you have had five husbands, and the*

*man you now have is not your husband. What you have just
said is quite true."*

*"Sir," the woman said, "I can see that you are a prophet.
Our fathers worshiped on this mountain, but you Jews claim
that the place where we must worship is in Jerusalem."*

*Jesus declared, "Believe me, woman, a time is coming when
you will worship the Father neither on this mountain nor in
Jerusalem. You Samaritans worship what you do not know;
we worship what we do know, for salvation is from the Jews.
Yet a time is coming and has now come when the true worshipers will worship the Father in spirit and truth, for they
are the kind of worshipers the Father seeks. God is spirit, and
his worshipers must worship in spirit and in truth."*

*The woman said, "I know that Messiah" (called Christ) "is
coming. When he comes, he will explain everything to us."*

Then Jesus declared, "I who speak to you am he."[9]

Would it have been loving for Jesus to have ignored the
truth of the woman's situation? Should he have validated her
"lifestyle choice"? Did he act wrongly by attempting to show the
woman the errors in her ways?

Of course not! The loving thing to do was exactly what Jesus
did. He did not ignore the truth but sensitively showed that Samaritan woman the truth of her situation and, in so doing, in-
troduced her to the Messiah (and, presumably, to new life).

It has been said that hate is not the true opposite of love; indifference is. If you *love* someone, you will not keep quiet about his
drug addiction, will you? You will not avoid the subject of her involvement in a dangerous cult, right? You will not ignore his destructive sexual behavior or the condition of her soul, will you? If
you love a person, you will not act indifferently toward dangerous

or destructive beliefs or behavior simply to avoid offending him or her. Yet the new tolerance demands just that sort of indifference.

Tolerance says, "You must agree with me." Love responds, "I must do something harder; I will tell you the truth because I am convinced that 'the truth will set you free.'"

Tolerance says, "You must approve of what I do." Love responds, "I must do something harder; I will love you, even when your behavior offends me."

Tolerance says, "You must allow me to have my way." Love responds, "I must do something harder; I will plead with you to follow the right way, because I believe you are worth the risk."

Tolerance seeks to be inoffensive; love takes risks. Tolerance is indifferent; love is active. Tolerance costs nothing; love costs everything.

Once again, Jesus is the supreme example of true Christian love, which is sometimes the antithesis of tolerance. His love drove him to a cruel death on the cross. Far from being indifferent to the "lifestyle choices" of others, he paid the price of those choices with his own life, and lovingly paved the way for everyone to "go, and sin no more" (John 8:11, KJV).

Love Won't Minister Condemnation

Another example of what real love won't do is this: Love won't minister condemnation. It won't leave a person feeling condemned but will offer hope of forgiveness and restoration.

If anyone had the right to condemn sinners, it was Jesus. He was perfect, without sin. Yet, "God did not send his Son into the world to condemn the world, but to save the world" (John 3:17). Do you remember his encounter with the woman caught in adultery?

> *The teachers of the law and the Pharisees brought in a woman caught in adultery. They made her stand before the group and said to Jesus, "Teacher, this woman was caught in the act of adultery. In the Law Moses commanded us to stone such women. Now what do you say?" They were using this question as a trap, in order to have a basis for accusing him.*
>
> *But Jesus bent down and started to write on the ground with his finger. When they kept on questioning him, he straightened up and said to them, "If any one of you is without sin, let him be the first to throw a stone at her." Again he stooped down and wrote on the ground.*
>
> *At this, those who heard began to go away one at a time, the older ones first, until only Jesus was left, with the woman still standing there. Jesus straightened up and asked her, "Woman, where are they? Has no one condemned you?"*
>
> *"No one, sir," she said.*
>
> *"Then neither do I condemn you," Jesus declared. "Go now and leave your life of sin."*[10]

Notice that Jesus differentiated between the woman and her behavior. And while he did not ignore her sin (commanding her to abandon her "life of sin"), he communicated love and mercy to her, not condemnation ("Neither do I condemn you").

This is what real love looks like. John Stott, writing on Romans 2:1-2 in his book *Romans: God's Good News for the World*, warns that Christians are not expected "either to suspend our critical faculties or to renounce all criticism and rebuke of others as illegitimate; [we are, however, prohibited from] standing in judgment on other people and condemning them (which as human beings we have no right to do), especially when we fail to condemn ourselves."[11]

It is that very approach that we must reclaim if we ever hope to love as Jesus loves. We must consciously and consistently distinguish between *the person* and *the person's beliefs, behavior, lifestyle, and truth claims.* We must communicate Christlike love and acceptance for the person *even if* we disagree with that person's beliefs or abhor that person's behavior. And we must neither ignore the truth of that person's situation *nor* minister condemnation to him or her. This distinction allows us to strike the biblical balance of aggressively living in love while humbly standing for truth.

Aggressively live in love	Humbly stand for truth
"You are my brother or sister, worthy of my loving acceptance and respect as an unimaginably valuable human being created in the image of God, a priceless soul for whom Christ died."	"Because I love you, I will humbly point to the truth about anything that threatens your happiness, health, and spiritual well-being."

Notice that I suggest we *aggressively* live in love and *humbly* stand for truth. It is important to keep the two approaches straight. We must be aggressive in pursuing love because love is our commission; it is our great cause, our "secret weapon" for winning the hearts of men and women to the Lord Jesus Christ. At the same time, however, we must not neglect to stand for truth.

Not long ago, a student writing for a college newspaper defended the homosexual agenda, saying:

> I suppose I can imagine what it would be like to believe
> that homosexuality is morally wrong (that makes me tol-

erant). But I think it's morally wrong to discriminate against people based on who they want to marry. . . .

Please don't send me hate mail quoting the "anti-gay" verses you all know—Jesus taught love before all else. Basically, all I ask from those . . . who disagree with a homosexual lifestyle is for them to allow people to determine their own values.[12]

There is much that could be said about that writer's appeal for "tolerance," but the comment that "Jesus taught love before all else" may be most revealing. Jesus taught love, *but never at the expense of truth* . . . because real love will not ignore the truth. His Word teaches that we should "love in the truth" (2 John 1:1) *and* "[speak] the truth in love" (Ephesians 4:15).

Yet I believe it is imperative to also be humble in seeking after and standing for truth because we do not have the authority within ourselves to judge right or wrong. Neither can we personally determine truth; we can only humbly point to what God says on the matter. When it comes right down to it, we *don't* have a corner on truth; but we can humbly—and lovingly—remind others that *God does.*

The problem is, Christians have too often failed to respond that way to people whose views are unbiblical or whose actions are immoral; we have too often stopped far short of the Christlike response of loving compassion and instead ministered condemnation of people's beliefs or behaviors. Instead of aggressively loving those who believe or behave differently than we do and humbly pointing them to the truth, we have tended to be restrained in expressing love and acceptance and arrogant in speaking truth, as though *we,* rather than God, had the authority to judge those outside the church (1 Corinthians 5:12-13). Yet, as Geevarghese Mar Osthathios has written:

In the final analysis, the Holy Spirit is the missionary convincing the world of sin, righteousness and judgement and we are asked to be *witnesses* of the crucified and risen Christ, not *judges* over others.[13]

So, what does this mean in practice? What does it look like in the real world? Once again, Jesus is our model. For instance, consider Luke's account of the Lord's encounter with Zacchaeus, in Luke 19:1-10:

> *Jesus entered Jericho and was passing through. A man was there by the name of Zacchaeus; he was a chief tax collector and was wealthy. He wanted to see who Jesus was, but being a short man he could not, because of the crowd. So he ran ahead and climbed a sycamore-fig tree to see him, since Jesus was coming that way.*
>
> *When Jesus reached the spot, he looked up and said to him, "Zacchaeus, come down immediately. I must stay at your house today." So he came down at once and welcomed him gladly.*
>
> *All the people saw this and began to mutter, "He has gone to be the guest of a 'sinner.'"*
>
> *But Zacchaeus stood up and said to the Lord, "Look, Lord! Here and now I give half of my possessions to the poor, and if I have cheated anybody out of anything, I will pay back four times the amount."*
>
> *Jesus said to him, "Today salvation has come to this house, because this man, too, is a son of Abraham. For the Son of Man came to seek and to save what was lost."*

Now, Zacchaeus was a sinner. He had lived a life of greed and extortion. Yet the scriptural account gives no indication that Jesus spoke any word of criticism or condemnation to Zacchaeus. He could have, of course; Jesus was God incarnate and had every right to point a finger at the man's conduct. But there is no indication he did.

Notice what Jesus did instead. He said, "Zacchaeus, come down immediately. I must stay at your house today." He communicated loving acceptance by expressing a desire to spend the day with the tax collector.

Notice, too, how Zacchaeus responded to Jesus' acceptance of him (though not his conduct). Zacchaeus broached the subject of his own sin: "Look, Lord! Here and now I give half of my possessions to the poor, and if I have cheated anybody out of anything, I will pay back four times the amount."

You see, Jesus did not minister condemnation to Zacchaeus; he didn't have to. Zacchaeus's own conduct condemned him, a fact that was no doubt driven home by the very presence of the sinless One. And, confronted with the presence of Jesus Christ, Zacchaeus admitted his sin, repented, and vowed to make restitution.

Of course, it is likewise important to notice that when Zacchaeus admitted his sin, Jesus did not contradict him. He did not say, "Oh, don't worry, Zacchaeus; you meant well." He didn't shrug his shoulders and say, "Hey, Zacchaeus, who am I to say that what you did was wrong?" He said, "Today salvation has come to this house." Jesus rejoiced that Zacchaeus had acknowledged his sin and repented.

Love Won't Neglect People's Needs

Jesus was considered a friend of sinners. He showed them acceptance by eating with them. He showed them comfort by healing their infirmities. He showed them attention by giving his time to them. He gained an audience with them because he looked beyond their sin and sought to meet their needs. Dr. David Ferguson, in his excellent book *The Great Commandment Principle*, helps us understand this crucial point:

> What happened in Jesus' incredible encounter with Zacchaeus? Paraphrasing a popular song from several years back, Jesus looked beyond his fault and saw his need. And when the love of Christ touched Zacchaeus at the point of his need, that love constrained the sinner to confess his sin and make things right. In other words, Christ's love ministered to the man's deep need, and Zacchaeus responded to that love by dealing with his own fault.
>
> If Jesus had simply rebuked Zacchaeus in the tree for his sinful behavior and gone his way, would the results have been the same? Probably not. No doubt Zacchaeus had been rebuked regularly by the religious leaders of the day, who were not about to defile themselves by fraternizing with him. Jesus, however, discerned the tax collector's needs as well as his dishonesty. Like everyone else, Zacchaeus needed attention, acceptance, respect, etc., but he was seeking to meet those needs in sinful ways. Once he experienced Christ's loving acceptance, Zacchaeus was ready to receive the truth about his sinful ways.[14]

That is the "more excellent way" to which Christians are called—a way to enter into a relationship with a needy world and offer it love and acceptance.

The living Christ bids us to enter into relationship with others—even those whose beliefs or behavior seem reprehensible to us—and, as he did with Zacchaeus, minister the love and acceptance of Christ toward them. It was the *presence of Christ* in relationship that showed Zacchaeus his sin and changed his life. Similarly, the Lord wants each of us to enter into real, loving, accepting relationships with those who don't know him, "for the Son of Man came to seek and to save what was lost" (Luke 19:10).

MISSION FIELD, NOT BATTLEFIELD

For too long, the primary Christian "outreach" method has consisted of inviting unchurched people to church. There's nothing wrong with that, of course, and many have been brought to salvation by such a simple invitation. But I strongly believe the Lord wants us to break out of our "Christian ghettos," seek out those with non-Christian beliefs, behaviors, and lifestyles, and invite them into our homes, eat with them, exercise with them, sit with them when they're sick, and expose them to the presence of Christ through his Holy Spirit who is alive in us.

The approach I am suggesting does not negate one-on-one evangelism; that is just as relevant as ever. Neither is it a substitute for teaching the truth; I have dedicated my life to telling the world the truth. What I am suggesting is a complement to "initiative evangelism," and the platform from which the truth can be more effectively told.

As Professor John D. Woodbridge has suggested:

We must remember that we serve a triune God who loves sinners: "For God so loved the world, that he gave his one and only Son." This familiar verse (John 3:16) reviews a marvelous display of God's salvific love. For "the world" we could substitute the rapist, the homosexual, the adulterer, the secular humanist, the capitalist robber-baron, the militarist war-monger. God really loves these people. He loved them so much that he gave his only begotten Son for them. And we are to love them as well, even while we know that sin is truly grievous to God (Pss. 5:6-7; 7:11; Malachi 1:3). . . .

If we see the world through our Lord's eyes, tender with compassion, we will be wary of putting on the culture-war spectacles of "us against them." Moreover, [we will] see our neighborhood or local school not as another battlefield in the "culture war" but as a mission field. Our home and church do not become military bunkers but havens of hospitality with the sign "Welcome" displayed over the front doors.[15]

The new tolerance requires people to accept all beliefs and behavior as legitimate and worthy of approval and even participation; true Christian love will go much further. It will attempt to recognize the relational needs behind a person's belief or behavior, just as Jesus looked beyond Zacchaeus's fault and saw his need (something the Lord has done for each of us). Too often, we Christians tend to recognize only people's spiritual needs; "They just need Jesus," we say. But many "wrong beliefs" and "sinful behaviors" are expressions of a deeper relational or emotional hurt. While every sinner does need the Savior, we must not neglect the deep relational needs that must often be addressed before a non-Christian can even respond to Christ's love and grace.

For example, several years ago, I agreed to speak at an outdoor high school assembly in Phoenix, Arizona. As I stood on a large rock to speak to the crowd of about a thousand students, a group of punk rockers, sporting fluorescent hair and wearing yards of chains, walked up to within twenty feet of where I stood. Some of the teachers and other students kept watchful eyes on the colorful group, expecting them to cause some kind of disturbance, but I continued my talk and finished speaking without interruption. As soon as I had finished speaking and stepped down off the rock, however, the apparent leader of the wildly dressed group ran up and planted himself less than a foot in front of my face. A gasp arose from the crowd, and five hundred pairs of eyes seemed to be trained on me and that young man.

The majority of the crowd, however, couldn't see the tears that streamed down the punk rocker's face, nor could they hear him asking me to hug him. But a wave of murmurs rolled through the crowd as I threw my arms around that young man and he buried his head in my shoulder and cried. The hug lasted about a minute—a long hug for a punk rocker! Finally, he let go of me and through tears explained, "My father never once hugged me or said, 'I love you.'"

Now, did that young man have spiritual needs? Did he need to experience salvation in Christ? Absolutely. But he had relational needs too. He was crying out for love and acceptance, and his outlandish appearance and wild behavior were a cry for attention and affection. And because I was able to demonstrate my own attention and affection, he allowed me to share the love of God in Christ with him, leading him to surrender his life to Jesus.

If we hope to counter the rise of the new tolerance, we must begin to recognize the relational needs that prompt the teenagers in our neighborhood to dress in such outlandish ways; we need to understand the needs that cause the homosexual activists in our cities to shout so loudly for acceptance and approval; we need to focus on the needs that provoke militant feminists to march for abortion on demand; we need to respond to the needs of young people who reject our values and seek to do "their own thing."

I am convinced that as Christians begin to sincerely befriend even the most militant homosexuals, the most dedicated abortionists, or the most hardened criminals and recognize and respond to their relational needs, the appeal of the new tolerance will begin to pale in the light of true Christian love.

I am convinced that as Christian students strive to show extra-mile kindness to professors who are antagonistic to the faith, the charm of the new tolerance will seem shallow compared to the power of true Christian love.

I am convinced that as Christians set the standard, as we once did, in racial reconciliation and unity, the influence of the new tolerance will be lost in the shadow of true Christian love.

I am convinced that as Christians brighten the darkest corners of human belief and behavior with the light of the love of Christ—building relationships and responding to the deepest relational needs of those trapped in sin—that *we* and *our children* and *our churches* will not only escape the dangers of the new tolerance ourselves; we will also "shine like stars" in the midst of "a crooked and depraved generation" (Philippians 2:15).

Chapter 7

TOLERANCE AND EDUCATION

My son Sean was a high school senior when I asked, "Son, in twelve years of school, were you ever taught any absolute truth?"

"Sure," he said.

Surprised, I asked, "What absolute truth have you learned in public schools?"

He shrugged. "Tolerance," he said.

I must admit that I was surprised then. But no longer. A generation or more ago, schools focused on such subjects as English, history, math, and science; today, one of the primary goals of many educators—at the primary, secondary, and college levels—is to teach and promote the new tolerance, as the following story illustrates:

Shawna stood at the front door, packed and ready to leave for the weekend with her friend Terilyn.

"When do you get home from this conference thing with Terilyn?" her mother asked her, fluffing her hair as she spoke.

"It's a three-day conference," Shawna answered. "We'll be back Sunday evening about six."

"And what is this conference exactly?"

Shawna had told her mother about the conference before, but not "exactly." If Shawna had told everything, her mother would have freaked out and quickly slammed the door on the whole weekend. "Young Women's Leadership Conference at the Hilton in San Francisco," she answered. "Terilyn says it's the best way to get into the student government at Reagan High School. The student council advisor is taking ten girls from Reagan, and Terilyn got me in."

It was all true. But what Shawna was *not* telling her mother was that a major unit planned for the conference was on tolerance.

After checking into the downtown Hilton the next day, Shawna and Terilyn went for pizza with Reagan's student advisor, Lisa Carmona. They were discussing the topics of the conference listed in the program, when one of the other students said that she sometimes got confused when people talked about tolerance. She wasn't sure what it really meant sometimes.

"Tolerance is the highest of all virtues," Ms. Carmona said, smiling. "It is the highest virtue because it acknowledges and celebrates the personal rights and values of all cultures and peoples. But it is often misunderstood because the fundamentalists in our culture have improperly defined it."

Ms. Carmona twirled her soda straw between her manicured fingers. "The virtue of tolerance is based on the reality that everyone is equal in value. Nobody at this table is better than anyone else, right?" The girls nodded as if on cue. "That's right. We're different from each other in a lot of ways, but we're all equal in value. And if all cultures and all persons are equal in value, then all lifestyles are equal. Tolerance is simply accepting and respecting another person's beliefs and lifestyle choices."

Shawna nodded along with the other girls. She suspected that her mom—and her pastor, probably—would find something wrong with Ms. Carmona's ideas, but Shawna sure couldn't find any fault with them. After all, Ms. Carmona was a teacher; she obviously knew what she was talking about.[1]

Shawna's fictional experience, drawn from the novel *Vote of Intolerance,* is typical of the experiences of many of our children in public schools and universities today, from grade-school children to grad students. The message of the new tolerance is having a profoundly negative effect on the education system—and, more important, on our children. There are six major areas that are being negatively affected. The new tolerance is stifling scholastic achievement, devaluing educational substance, rewriting history, ignoring facts, restricting freedoms, and denying parental rights. Short of complete isolation, how can we respond to the influence of the new tolerance on our education systems? How can we diminish the new tolerance's negative effects on our children and on their education?

First and foremost, we must apply the "more excellent way" in each situation. Remember that Christians are called to be "the salt of the earth" and "the light of the world" (Matthew 5:13, 14). A loving response does not require that we compromise or capitulate to our culture regarding what is best for our children. Neither does it require that we engage in a "holy war" with the education system. A well-informed Christian exercising Christlike love can counter the culture effectively by adopting a "wise as serpents and harmless as doves" approach (Matthew 10:16, KJV).

THE DOMINANT THEME OF THE MODERN CURRICULUM

"We share a world. For all our differences of politics, race, economics, abilities, culture and language—we share one world. To be tolerant is to welcome the differences and delight in the sharing."[2]

So begins the introduction to the Web-site homepage of *Teaching Tolerance* magazine, a publication that is offered free to schoolteachers and administrators by the Southern Poverty Law Center. "Tolerance can be taught," editor Sara Bullard writes, "not just talked about. Teachers have developed an astounding variety of techniques that work, and we'll share them with you. . . . Tolerance is an idea that is universally relevant, and it belongs everywhere in the curriculum. Here you will read about teachers and students working together to improve race relations, respect religious diversity and ability differences, dispel gender bias and homophobia, confront hate and build classroom community."[3]

Don't miss the importance of Bullard's claims. "Tolerance . . . *belongs everywhere in the curriculum.*" This means, practically speaking, that the new tolerance should be taught in history classes, art classes, science classes—even math classes! In fact, the National Council of Social Studies (NCSS), in its 1992 "Curriculum Guidelines for Multicultural Education," claims

that "education for multiculturalism [which is the new tolerance applied to diverse cultures] . . . requires more than a
change in curricula and textbooks. It requires systemwide
changes that permeate all aspects of school."[4] This goal of teaching tolerance everywhere extends to the university as well. According to Kenneth S. Stern, "Teaching diversity should be an
educational mission that saturates the campus."[5] And Stephen
Bates, writing in *The American Enterprise*, sums it all up with
these chilling words:

> Tolerance may indeed be the dominant theme of the mod-
> ern curriculum. The authors of a recent study of American
> high schools concluded "tolerating diversity is the moral
> glue that holds schools together." One study of American
> history books found toleration presented as "the only 'reli-
> gious' idea worth remembering."[6]

Not only is tolerance often considered the only " 'religious'
idea worth remembering," but the new tolerance appears to be
the only virtue that many consider worthy of inclusion in school
curriculums. Consider the following statement, made by the
top official of the New Hampshire chapter of the National Education Association to George W. Fellendorf, chairman of New
Hampshire's Christian Coalition and a specialist in education,
at a recent education forum in that state:

> If children come to school with different values than those
> they are taught at school, teachers should encourage the
> kids to discard the lessons their parents are teaching.[7]

Frightening, isn't it? Yet that is precisely what *must* happen
and what *is* happening in this era of the new tolerance, at the

primary, secondary, and post-secondary levels. Throughout the U.S., Canada, and other Western nations, books and classes are being revised to make schools more "inclusive," more "diverse," more "sensitive," "gender neutral," "antiracist," and "disability aware." Some of the changes are positive. It is good for students to learn not only about William Shakespeare and George Washington but also about Sequoya (the inventor of the Cherokee alphabet), Martin Luther King Jr., and Gandhi. It is good for us all to learn from the often-neglected music, literature, drama, and customs of other cultures.

Unfortunately, however, the agenda of the new tolerance is far deeper—and darker—than simply exposing schoolchildren to other cultures. Even at the primary and secondary levels, the proponents of new tolerance are carrying on a campaign of indoctrination that is most noticeable and most dangerous in six areas.

Sacrificing Achievement for Self-Esteem

As we've stated before, the new tolerance asserts not only that all cultures are equal but also that a person's identity is inextricably linked with his or her culture. Therefore, if students are to be treated "tolerantly," they must be consciously treated and educated as members of their specific racial, ethnic, or even sexual-orientation group. Only then, it is reasoned, will they begin to develop the self-esteem that is thought necessary to academic achievement.

In reality, however, the development of self-esteem often eclipses learning goals in schools dominated by the new tolerance. Real achievement is often sacrificed in order not to harm students' self-esteem. For example, Richard Bernstein, in his book *Dictatorship of Virtue: Multiculturalism and the Battle for America's Future*, records the account of a seminar conducted by a multiculturalist consultant:

> McIntosh [the consultant] begins with a story. She was recently in Roxbury, she says, referring to Boston's predominantly poor, black neighborhood, where she watched as a young black child attempted to cope with a math work sheet involving the addition of twenty-four sets of three single-digit numbers, like 2+4+3.
> "She was trying to get these problems right," McIntosh said. "The alternative was to get them wrong." But the girl didn't understand the math involved; she got the first problem wrong and got the others wrong also. . . . "So this is a situation within the win-lose world in which there's no way the child can feel good about the assignment."[8]

Bernstein goes on to describe the consultant's suggestions for helping the child "feel good about the assignment," but he notes that McIntosh *never suggested a solution to the girl's inability to do sums* and apparently avoided any suggestion that the student's self-esteem might be improved by true learning and achievement!

Lynn Cheney, former chairperson of the National Endowment for the Humanities under Presidents Reagan and Bush, writes:

> Education is about the pursuit of truth, and one of the characteristics of [the new tolerance] is that it turns education into something else—a procedure for making people feel good, for example; a way of building self-esteem. . . . Education is not primartily about self-esteem.

It is about learning to seek evidence, to evaluate information, to weigh conflicting opinions.[9]

This characteristic of the new tolerance must concern all of us, regardless of our skin color. Far too many of our precious children and young people (of every race, color, and religion) are neither learning nor achieving because their education system is turning many of their teachers into social workers, whose primary goal is not to educate but to help their students "feel good about the assignment."

But Christians *can* make a difference, particularly if we make every effort to

- Lovingly challenge the notion that a person's identity is inseparable from his or her culture. Instead, promote the biblical basis for self-esteem; that is, that men, women, and children should be respected—and should respect themselves—not because they are members of a specific racial, ethnic, or sexual-orientation group, but because they are the unique and wonderful work of God (Psalm 139:13-14).

- Concentrate on loving and accepting people (of every race, color, and religion) *regardless* of what they do because who they are *does not equal* what they do. Help students experience love and acceptance whether they bring home D's or A's on their report cards, even while you encourage more effort if that is necessary.

- Defend *every* child's right to learn. Tactfully challenge curricula that do not prepare students—of every race and religion—to demonstrate competence in an increasingly competitive global economy.

Sacrificing Substance for Style

Walk down the halls of most primary and secondary schools in the U.S. and Canada today and you will likely encounter a stimulating kaleidoscope of posters, mobiles, and other teaching aids bearing such titles as "Great Moments in Black History" and "American-Indian Women in Mathematics" and a "Peace Wall" honoring such peacemakers as Gandhi, Martin Luther King Jr., and Chief Joseph of the Nez Percé. These days, schoolchildren and high school students are learning about such previously neglected cultures as the Ashanti and Yoruba cultures of Africa and the Zuni and Ojibwa cultures of North America. In Queens, New York, students of Asian descent have been placed in bilingual classrooms *against the wishes of their parents,* who would prefer that their children learn in English, like non-Asian students.[10]

Unfortunately, however, this "multicultural smorgasbording" of public education usually has the effect not only of adding to a student's knowledge but of subtracting as well. There are, after all, only so many hours in a school day, and many subjects are chosen not because they are valuable or useful but because they represent this culture or that culture. As a result, such important figures as William Shakespeare and George Washington are often crowded out, along with such important events as the defeat of the Spanish Armada and the invention of the airplane and such important documents as the Magna Carta and the U.S. Constitution.

Bernstein relates a conversation with a teacher of fifth and sixth graders in which he asked what she taught her students about George Washington. "That he was the first president," she answered, "that he was a slave owner, that he was rich—not much."[11]

Consequently, many of our children and youth are gaining a vast knowledge of multicultural facts; but at the same time we have, according to education activist Candace de Russy, "seriously eroded the core competencies we used to take for granted. Now we have college students graduating as cultural illiterates—and some total illiterates. And graduates without a command of English."[12] This disparity doesn't concern many "tolerant" educators, however, because in the world of the new tolerance, educational substance is generally not as important as students' learning about other lifestyles and feeling good about who they are.

We must be concerned about the substitution of style for substance. And we can make a difference, particularly if our concern takes the following shapes:

- Parents, remember that *you,* not their teachers, not their principals, and not their school or school board, are in charge of your children's education. Pay attention to what they are being taught; browse through their textbooks; drop into an occasional assembly; chaperon a field trip now and then. Express any concerns in a gracious but firm manner, and make an extra effort to express appreciation when the school or teacher shows sensitivity to or support for your rights as a parent.
- In the same vein, don't wait for the school to introduce your child to substance in education. Ask your children at mealtimes what they know about George Washington *and* George Washington Carver, about Martin Luther *and* Martin Luther King Jr.
- If possible, graciously offer your assistance to teachers in areas that are important to you. For example, if your

child's history text discusses only your nation's guilty participation in slavery, offer to present a class or two on the greatness of those who fought for abolition (such as William Wilberforce in the British Empire and Frederick Douglass in the U.S.).

Sacrificing History for Propaganda

Another dangerous effect of the new tolerance in public schools and universities today is the systematic replacement of history with propaganda. Two historians from the University of Pennsylvania boldly admit as much, writing:

> We are all engaged in writing a kind of propaganda. . . . Rather than believe in the absolute truth of what we are writing, we must believe in the moral and political position we are taking with it. . . . Historians should assess an argument on the basis of its persuasiveness, its political utility, and its political sincerity.[13]

In other words, many of those who are writing history today no longer feel a need to be accurate; instead, they aim for political persuasiveness. They are asking not, "Is it the truth?" but, "Is it politically useful?" As Gene Edward Veith puts it, "Since there is no objective truth, history may be rewritten according to the needs of a particular group. . . . Truth does not have to get in the way."[14] And, indeed, much of the so-called history and culture being taught by proponents of the new tolerance betrays a fourfold agenda:

(1) Take the West down a peg,

(2) Romanticize non-Western, nontraditional, non-White cultures,

(3) Treat all cultural values as equal,

(4) Refrain from criticizing non-Western, nontraditional, non-White cultures.[15]

"Liberal arts students," writes Dinesh D'Souza, author and research fellow at the American Enterprise Institute, "including those attending Ivy League schools, are very likely to be exposed to an attempted brainwashing that deprecates Western learning and exalts a neo-Marxist ideology promoted in the name of multiculturalism. Even students who choose hard sciences . . . are almost certain to be inundated with an anti-Western, anti-capitalistic view of the world."[16] D'Souza is hardly the only scholar saying such things; even Eugene Genovese, a Marxist historian, has admitted (with regret) the fact that "education has given way to indoctrination" in our schools today.[17]

Bernstein illustrates this by citing a high school course called "World in Crisis" at Brookline High School in an affluent suburb of Boston. The course focused on three crisis areas: Northern Ireland, the Middle East, and Vietnam. Bernstein writes:

> The choice [of those three crisis areas] as the only areas of study in the course is rather curious. Why not the Soviet Union in Afghanistan, or 1968 in Czechoslovakia? Why not the Cold War or Khomeini's Iran or Islamic funda-mentalism, or the civil war in Lebanon or in Burundi, or the dissolution of the Soviet Union, if teachers are inter-ested in portraying the world in crisis?
>
> "The section on Northern Ireland showed the British as the villains, the Indochina part showed America as the villain, then the part on the Mideast ended up implying

that the problem was a sinister one of oppression of Palestinians by European colonists," [reported Sandra Stotsky, one parent who studied the course]. . . . "By the time students finish this course, they have been implicitly encouraged to see all white Protestants, Americans, the British, other Europeans, and Israelis as oppressors of the poor or people of color and to view Britain, America, and Israel, all democracies, as the major oppressor nations of the world."[18]

This agenda is not confined to colleges and universities. Its success is apparent in the comment of one fifth-grade teacher to Richard Bernstein: "The sentiment in my [class]room is that they don't like Christians and they don't like white people because they saw what has been done in the name of Christianity and what the white people did to the Indians and the Africans."[19]

There is, of course, much in the history of the church and in the history of the United States and other Western nations that should and must be acknowledged and condemned, but the Spanish Inquisition and America's Indian wars and slave trade hardly present a complete picture of church history and American history. Yet that is virtually the only picture some students are shown in this age of the new tolerance, and it is producing a bumper crop of anti-Christian and anti-American sentiment, leading Albert Shanker of the American Federation of Teachers to comment, "No other nation in the world teaches a national history that leaves its children feeling negative about their own country—this would be the first."[20]

This substitution of propaganda for history can be countered, however, if we seek to do the following in love:

• Advocate true appreciation for other cultures, not because all cultural practices are equal (though all cultures
do possess both positive and negative aspects), but because all cultures illustrate the unity of the human condition (we are all sinners in need of God's redeeming
power) and our instinctive approval of virtue and dis-
dain for vice . . . not only in other cultures but in our
own as well. Regardless of your skin color or ethnic
background, discover the inspiring stories of Booker T.
Washington and Sojourner Truth, the tragic experiences
of Chief Joseph's Nez Percé tribe and the Kurds of Saddam Hussein's Iraq, the delicate *shan-shui* landscapes of
ancient China and the architectural achievements of the
Mayan and Aztec cultures. Condemn the slavery that existed in nineteenth-century America no less than that
which exists in Sudan today.

Take advantage of every opportunity to cross racial
and cultural lines, and demonstrate the Spirit of Christ,
"who crossed religious, gender and ethnic lines in order to
heal and teach."[21] Never hesitate to worship with Christians from other racial, ethnic, or cultural backgrounds.
"If there are any cultural barriers existing among different
ethnic groups," writes Peter Tze Ming Ng of the Chinese
University of Hong Kong, "it is the church's mission to
demonstrate that Christ has indeed broken these dividing
walls."[22]

• Don't fall into the trap of looking at the Christian
church as a White and Western institution, as Peter Tze
Ming Ng points out:

Christians believe that Christ was crucified, died, and

was resurrected for people of every culture and race. If one really believes that Christ is the Savior of all humankind, then one has to affirm that Christ is also the Savior of one's Asian, African, Hispanic, and Native American neighbors. They are not merely marginal Christians but belong to the same family of God. The Book of Galatians has much relevance for Christians today when Paul says, "It is through faith that all of you are God's sons in union with Christ Jesus. . . . There is no difference between Jews and Gentiles, between slaves and free men, between men and women; you are all one in union with Christ Jesus."[23]

Take every opportunity to remind yourself and as many other people around you as possible that

The real church is—and always has been—multicultural. . . . [God] made his church multicultural, and it was his intention from the beginning that it be so. . . .

When we think of the church we must conjure up a picture not of people like ourselves, but of people of all colors and shapes and ages, women and men speaking different tongues, following different customs, practicing different habits, but all worshiping the same Lord.[24]

That needs to be our vision of the church, and we need to help educators and others recognize that reality as well.

- Help others understand that each of us is responsible for his or her own sins (Deuteronomy 24:16; Ezekiel 18:20); we can learn from the sins of past generations, perhaps even correct their effects, but we cannot cleanse them or atone for them. We are responsible for our own misdeeds, but here also is a message of deliverance that even the proponents of the new tolerance (including teachers and professors, principals and deans) need to hear: "If we confess our sins, he is faithful and just and will forgive us our sins and purify us from all unrighteousness" (1 John 1:9).

Sacrificing Fact for Fiction

Not only does the new tolerance include propaganda that is antagonistic toward Christianity and Western culture and civilization, in addition to romanticizing propaganda favorable to other cultures; it sometimes purposely *invents* propaganda favorable to other cultures, as evidenced by the passionate statement of Stanford undergraduate William King, president of the Black Student Union:

> Under the old system, he said, "I was never taught . . . the fact that Socrates, Herodotus, Pythagoras and Solon studied in Egypt and acknowledged that much of their knowledge of astronomy, geometry, medicine and building came from the African civilization in and around Egypt. [I was never taught] that the Hippocratic Oath acknowledges the Greeks' 'father of medicine,' Imhotep, a black Egyptian pharoah whom they called Aesculapius. . . . I was never informed when it was found that the 'very dark and wooly haired' Moors in Spain preserved, expanded and reintroduced the classical knowledge that the Greeks had collected, which led to the 'renaissance.' . . . I read the Bible without knowing Saint Augustine looked black like me, that the Ten Commandments were almost direct copies from the 147 Negative Confessions of Egyptian initiates. . . . I didn't learn Toussaint L'Ouverture's defeat of

Napoleon in Haiti directly influenced the French Revolution, or that the Iroquois Indians in America had a representative democracy which served as a model for the American system."[25]

"This statement," writes D'Souza, "drew wild applause and was widely quoted. The only trouble is that much of it is untrue. There is no evidence that Socrates, Pythagoras, Herodotus and Solon studied in Egypt, although Herodotus may have traveled there. Saint Augustine was born in North Africa, but his skin color is unknown, and in any case he could not have been mentioned in the Bible; he was born over 350 years after Christ. Viewing King's speech at my request, Bernard Lewis, an expert in Islamic and Middle Eastern culture at Princeton, described it as 'a few scraps of truth amidst a great deal of nonsense.'"[26]

Such dubious claims[27] may be the wave of the future in public education, however, like the claims of Dr. Leonard Jeffries, the head of African-American studies at City College of New York. Jeffries' claims include the "discoveries" that concentrations of melanin give blacks superior intelligence, that Caucasians are "ice people" who are genetically predisposed to meanness and aggression, and that AIDS was created as part of a conspiracy by Whites to destroy Blacks.[28]

Those views are as baseless as those that claim that the European and Western heritage is the repository of *all* that is good and worthwhile in culture. No! It must be said, and adamantly so, that there is much in the cultural heritage of Black, Asian, Hispanic, and Native American students that should be taught and appreciated by students of all races. But letter writer D. Jackson, commenting on his Afrocentric education in a California school, was right to argue that *inventing* history is a betrayal, not a defense, of Black pride. "We should stop lying to ourselves and our children, and stop concocting a false racial résumé," he said. "Are we so ashamed of our history that we have to start claiming other peoples' achievements as our own?"[29]

Perhaps most disturbing, however, is the fact that the dubious nature of such claims means nothing to the proponents of the new tolerance and multiculturalism because the point, to them, is not truth but power. If propagating "a false racial résumé" serves to shift power in any way from the so-called dominant culture (i.e., White, Christian, European) to another culture, then (they reason) it should be done . . . in the name of tolerance.

But Christians need not play along with such tactics. In fact, we have a message of hope for those who are tempted to sacrifice fact for fiction in the name of the new tolerance:

- Strive, in such situations as those described above, to exalt truth instead of power, fact over fiction, documentation rather than speculation (and teach your children to do the same). Learn to ask politely, "Can you tell me how you know that?" "Where did you learn that?" "Can you offer any support for your view?"
- Seek to widen your sphere of friends and acquaintances as much as possible. It is easier to pursue "the more excellent way" in sensitive areas (such as race, power, and politics, for example) when you can hear other perspectives firsthand. This will help you to "seek first to understand, then to be understood."

Sacrificing Freedom for "Political Correctness"

Not long ago I was speaking at Fishnet, a music festival in Virginia, when eight different students came up to me and verified what I was saying about the education system. "Everything you're talking about," they said, "we're experiencing. In fact, at our university, if you're accused of intolerance, you have to take a class in cultural sensitivity in order to graduate." One of the students added, "I'm very committed to Jesus, but this has been the hardest year of my life. I'm an R.A. [resident advisor], and last year I had to attend a two-day conference on tolerance. They brought in gays, lesbians, pedophiles, and they said we must be tolerant and accepting. They said, 'You have to learn to determine what is right for you and what is wrong for you. No one can do that for you, and you cannot impose your values upon others. You must allow others the freedom to determine what is right and wrong for them, and then live it out unhindered.' Every session they start out by telling us, 'You can't change anyone. If you try you will be fired and it will go down as a permanent mark on your record.' I'm at the place now where I'm afraid to mention the name of Jesus Christ, even in the privacy of my own room; any accusation that I was trying to convert someone would cause tremendous problems."

Such infringement of individual freedoms is common also in some primary and secondary schools, where prayer and the mention of Jesus Christ are considered unacceptable—even criminal—behavior. Consider the following cases:

- An eleven-year-old boy was forbidden to recite a poem in school because it contained a reference to Jesus.
- A young Pennsylvania student was told it was inappropriate to write "Jesus Loves You" on a lunch box.
- High school students in Texas were banned from advertising their after-school Bible club unless they omitted the names of God and Jesus.[30]

Remember, such things are allowed to occur because Christ and Christianity represent an intolerant, absolutist, dogmatic view to the proponents of the new tolerance. Therefore, any intolerance toward Christians is considered good and proper.

Furthermore, the willingness of those who promote the new tolerance to persecute those who don't play along is perhaps nowhere more evident than in education. For example, the Department of Residential Living at the University of Pennsylvania issues a written notice to all resident advisors, grad students, and faculty who live in undergrad dorms:

> [The notice] tells them not only to behave well but that even if they are "perceived" to harbor impure attitudes, they are ipso facto guilty of "an attitude of intolerance. . . ."
>
> "If you are *perceived* to be racist, sexist, heterosexist, ethnocentric, biased against those with religions different from your own, or intolerant of disabilities, you must be willing to examine and change that behavior," the administration's notice says. [italics added][31]

Some universities, such as the University of Michigan and the University of Connecticut, have attempted to adopt aggressive "speech codes," intended to eradicate such things as "inappropriately directed laughter, inconsiderate jokes, anonymous notes or phone calls, and the conspicuous exclusion of another student from conversation."[32]

Today "intolerance" is considered so evil by some that it justifies denial of a person's right to free speech (such as simply mentioning the name of Christ) and extends even to how you laugh or whom you exclude from a conversation.

So, what does "the more excellent way" of Christlike love look like in an education system that sacrifices basic freedoms in the name of the new tolerance? It will certainly include (but not be limited to) the following:

- First, "let your conversation be always full of grace, seasoned with salt" (Colossians 4:6). "Do not let any unwholesome talk come out of your mouths" but "[speak] the truth *in love,*" as the Bible says (Ephesians 4:29; 4:15, italics added). Make sure that if you are persecuted or any of your freedoms are infringed, it is for righteousness' sake . . . and not because you have acted rudely or cruelly.

- Make the most of every opportunity to communicate loving acceptance of others, especially when you must take a stand for truth, and teach your children to do the same. For example, if a teacher or professor suggests that "homosexuals are people too, so we cannot condemn homosexuality," the "more excellent way" might include raising a hand and saying, "I agree [that] homosexuals are infinitely valuable in God's eyes, just like all of us," before any discussion of the wrongness of homosexual behavior.

- Know your rights and the rights of your children and other students. For example, Jay Sekulow and Keith Fournier, in their book, *And Nothing but the Truth,* point out that the following rights are protected by the U.S. Constitution, as affirmed in recent Supreme Court decisions:

- Bible clubs and religious organizations have the right to advertise on campus. Public-address systems, bulletin

127

boards, school newspapers, and normal outlets that are available to other clubs to disseminate their message are open to you.

- Student-initiated religious groups are protected. Students may develop groups in order to spread the gospel on campus. Schools must allow students the freedom to start and attend their own meetings on school campuses when the students attend.

- The [U.S.] Supreme Court has made it clear that schools cannot treat Bible clubs or religious organizations differently than other noncurriculum clubs in any way. You have the full right to be treated like any other organization. School officials must give you the same meeting time as other groups and the same ability to get your message out as is provided to other students.

- You cannot be prohibited from wearing a shirt with a Christian message or any other message. This right is protected by the First Amendment. Students cannot be barred from bringing a Bible on campus or into the schoolroom. The student is bound only by an obligation not to disrupt school discipline.

- You have the right to share your faith in your high school. School officials cannot control student speech just because the particular speech is religious in nature. Students have the right to pass out papers, tracts, or any material that expresses their viewpoint to their peers. In the Mergens case,[33] the Court's opinion made it clear that a student's right to share his or her faith does not interfere with other students' rights.

- Your rights extend to the classroom, the cafeteria, and the playing field outside. You can surround the flagpole.

No one can keep you from praying silently wherever you choose. . . . When students gather as a group during their free time, they are guaranteed . . . basic rights, including corporate prayer.[34]

Sacrificing Parental Rights for Governmental Authority

An odd paradox exists in the public school systems of the United States. School nurses may not issue an aspirin to a student without parental permission, but school clinic personnel may freely and broadly distribute condoms without even notifying the parents. Similarly, teachers send home detailed permission slips (complete with medical information in case of an emergency) for their students to attend a field trip to the zoo, but in some states a minor can obtain an abortion without her parents' knowledge.

As a direct result of the postmodern influence, parents' rights to guide and influence their children's lives are being systematically undermined and overthrown. Consider the words of Paul Kurtz, a self-styled "humanist" and profesor of philosophy at State University of New York (SUNY) at Buffalo:

Parents have no right to impose their religion on their children or to prevent them from being exposed to other points of view. A Fundamentalist Protestant, an Orthodox Jewish, Roman Catholic, or Muslim parent has no right to expect the state to support his own narrow conception of education, particularly since we all share the same world culture.[35]

And columnist Robert Holland, writing of the so-called Magaziner Commission set up by the National Center on Education and the Economy, lists a series of goals the commission identified for schools, then adds, "Remarkably, parents were mentioned not once in this thick document. Rather, the report called for the school system to instill attitudes in children desired by governmental and industrial elitists."[36]

Increasingly, the educational agenda in today's schools reflects the sentiment of Massachusetts Chief Justice Paul Liacos, who ruled that public schools—even junior high schools—may distribute condoms to students regardless of parents' objections, and added, "Parents have no right to tailor public school programs to meet their individual religious or moral preferences."[37]

Public education in the West is becoming more and more antagonistic toward parents, and particularly toward parents who attempt to influence what their children are being taught. But Christians, contrary to what Paul Kurtz may say, have not only a right but a responsibility to influence and oversee their children's education. In fact, God's Word makes it clear that education should not be confined to the hours when school is in session but should be guided by parents and should involve every activity of life, even the most mundane (Deuteronomy 6:6-9).

In addition, Christians should be careful to

- Keep the lines of communication wide open. Prior to the entrance of the first baby boomers into the halls of academia, the majority of children had been educated in small neighborhood schools, which were often staffed by relatives and neighbors, and the curriculum reflected the community. When the baby boom's first wave hit first grade, however, the sudden demand for teachers and classroom space changed the complexion of public education. Students were herded into what authors H. Stephen Glenn and Jane Nelsen call "education factories"[38]—huge regional schools of large classes taught by teachers who didn't know these kids or their parents. As a result, a structure that had previously reinforced parents' efforts to instill traditional values in their children could no longer identify those values, let alone support them.

The problem is, few of us have adapted our behavior to that change. We send our children off to be educated by *people we don't know.*

Make every effort to adapt to that reality by working to build strong relationships with your children's teachers, principals, superintendents, school-board members, PTA presidents, and school janitors. Attend open houses. Ask for teachers' E-mail addresses. We must learn which teachers (and others) share our values and convictions and which do not—not so we may "get rid of" the wrong-minded individuals, but in order to better understand them and, when necessary, counter their influence and ideas.

- Look for opportunities to express kindness and appreciation toward teachers and administrators. Make it your goal to perform at least two loving acts for every criticism or concern you must express to a school official.

- Tactfully insist on being informed *and* consulted regarding your child's education. React firmly to any actions that restrict your God-given position as your child's number one teacher.

As you can see, countering the culture of new tolerance requires that you be well informed. It will undoubtedly require you to counter and offset with a biblical worldview the things your child may be learning at school. But as you instill within your child a deep love for the one true God and for those around him or her, you and your family can truly "shine like stars" in the midst of "a crooked and depraved generation" (Philippians 2:15).

Chapter 8

TOLERANCE AND GOVERNMENT

In today's era dominated by the new tolerance, Christians will do well to keep in mind the following facts about the Founder of our faith:

- From the moment of his birth, he was considered a political threat (Matthew 2:16-18);
- he and his earliest followers were members of an oft-oppressed people ruled by a colonial power;
- he was executed by the state (Matthew 27:27-31).

For centuries Christians around the world have been forced to follow in the steps of Jesus. They have been martyred. They have been imprisoned. They have faced persecution and discrimination. They have often come into conflict with government because, as Philip Yancey says, they "understood that their faith was not merely private and devotional; it had implications for all of society, affecting law, general morality, health, and human welfare."[1]

For much of the past two centuries, Christians in America, Canada, and other Western nations have enjoyed a general freedom from such conditions. But I believe that is changing and, indeed, already has changed to a large degree. Consider the words of Alan Keyes, former ambassador to the United Nations under President Ronald Reagan:

> Where do we find the most persecuted Christians in the world? Do we find them in China, where in spite of all, the flame burns brightly . . . and continues to shine out new light and make a place for God's truth? Do we find them in the Sudan? I don't think so. Because all those rulers who think they can crush out the flame of truth with all their physical brutality have been proven—down through . . . these two thousand years—that they are wrong; the truth marches on!
>
> . . . I find [the most persecuted Christians] in the classrooms of our government schools, where the assault is not upon the body, but the soul. I find it in the lies that are being told to our young people, as time and again, in place after place, they are trying to pretend that sexual perversion and promiscuity are the normal order of the day. I find it on the screens of our movie houses and on our television shows, where *the assault is not upon the body but upon the truth that shapes the soul.* . . . I find it in the homes and hearts of this country. Parents whose rights and obligations with respect to their children's care and upbringing and schooling are being violated every single day by *the erection of a structure of government authority that, though it stands on the separation of church and state, in fact seems to seek to drive moral judgment and faith out of our lives.*
>
> . . . And I find it in the sterile clinics, where abortion assassins carry out daily their murders of the innocent unborn, and with that stroke take not only the physical life

of a babe, but *the moral heart and soul of our country.* That I find to be persecution. [italics added][2]

The Christian consensus that once governed the public and private life of the United States and other Western nations has crumbled to the point that we no longer live in a post-Christian society; we live in an anti-Christian society, one in which the Christian faith is dismissed or ridiculed and Christians are considered suspect and their motives and behavior berated. As a result, Christians are increasingly faced with the challenge of living in two irreconcilable kingdoms.

A TALE OF TWO KINGDOMS

In one of their many attempts to trap Jesus, the Pharisees asked him whether or not they should pay taxes to Caesar. Jesus, upon showing them the picture of the emperor and the inscription on a Roman coin, answered, "Give to Caesar what is Caesar's, and to God what is God's" (Matthew 22:21). The wisdom of his reply left them "amazed."

I believe part of the reason they were so amazed at his answer was that, as always, Jesus saw beyond the surface issue and went to the heart of the matter. And the heart issue was then, as it is now and always has been, how does a Christian live victoriously in two kingdoms? For that is what we are called to do. Jesus said, in his great priestly prayer in John 17, that his followers are "*in* the world" (v. 11, italics added) but "not *of* the world" (v. 14, italics added). In other words, we live in a kingdom that is ruled by the devil, "the prince of this world" (John 12:31), but "our citizenship is in heaven" (Philippians 3:20). As Christians, we have the unique distinction of dual citizenship. We are temporary citizens of the country in which we now live, which is part of the devil's kingdom, and we are permanent citizens of heaven, the kingdom of God.

Two different kingdoms. Two different sets of standards. In many cases, those standards are similar enough that living in two kingdoms poses no serious problem. In other cases, however, we find the two sets of standards diametrically opposed—with us in the middle. How do we handle that?

Most believers are of one mind that under no circumstance do we compromise God's standards. But what exactly does that mean? And how and where do we draw the line?

Romans 13:1 clearly states, "Everyone must submit himself to the governing authorities, for there is no authority except that which God has established. The authorities that exist have been established by God." Elsewhere, however, the apostle Peter declares, "We must obey God rather than men!" (Acts 5:29).

These two verses instruct us to be law-abiding citizens of whatever country we live in *to the extent that the law of the land does not contradict the greater law of God.* For instance, we should stop at stop signs, drive according to the speed limit, and pay our taxes. But if a law of the land orders us to do something that God's Word prohibits—like suppressing the gospel because it is an "intolerant" message that proclaims moral absolutes and objective truth—we must peacefully disobey the lesser worldly law in order to be true to God's greater law. If we fail to make that distinction—and follow through on it—we commit a grievous error.

We are "in the world" but not "of the world." But *what does that mean,* practically speaking? That's a good question, one Christians have answered in various ways, with varying success:

- **Strict Separationists:** These people want a completely nonreligious state, with the separation of traditional religion from all civic matters.
- **Pluralistic Separationists:** Those who fall into this category advocate a "neutral state" but still allow religious values to influence government policy as long as the policy is considered a "public matter."
- **Institutional Separationists:** The goal here is a "theocentric state," with the government maintaining a "benevolent neutrality" toward Judeo-Christian religious institutions and values.
- **Nonpreferentialists:** Those who subscribe to this ideal believe that the government, although nonsectarian itself, maintains a strong interest in "preserving and fostering faith" in the best interests of the public and as a basis for morality.
- **Restorationists:** This group believes in actively working to restore Christianity to the status they believe it held in early America; they want to see the country become a "Christian nation" again.[3]

Although there are variations of opinion within all these positions, most Christians fall into one of these categories. Our purpose here is not to advocate or condemn any of these positions. But as Christians with dual citizenship, we should be the best possible models of that citizenship, even as we remember that our greatest and most lasting victory was achieved not in Washington or Ottawa or any of the world's capitals but on the cross of Calvary. That is the true reason God has called us to dual citizenship: so we may exercise the "ministry of reconciliation" given to us by Christ (2 Corinthians 5:18). And we do that by living and proclaiming the gospel of love and truth.

FLASH POINTS

In science, a flash point is the temperature at which vapors (such as gasoline fumes) ignite in the air when exposed to a flame. There are likewise a number of highly charged flash points that you, your children, or your church are likely to encounter in today's cultural climate. What should a Christian do when governmental politics and policy unite with the new tolerance in a combustible combination? What does real Christian love look like in such situations? And what does it mean to aggressively live in love while humbly standing for truth? Those are the questions we'll seek to answer as we look at the new tolerance as it affects issues of church and state, life and death, and marriage and sexuality.

Church and State

Because the gospel of Jesus Christ is an affront to the doctrine of the new tolerance (which claims that all beliefs, behaviors, and truth claims are equal), the government is repeatedly called upon by the proponents of the new tolerance (who often constitute a pervasive influence *in* the government) to cleanse our schools, towns, cities, states, and provinces of Christian voices and ideas.

For example, consider the flash point that ignited in the northeast Alabama town of Gadsden. In 1980, Roy Moore crafted a piece of wood to resemble two stone tablets and used a woodburning tool to etch the Ten Commandments into the plaque. He displayed the plaque in his home and then later in his law office. When he became a district judge in 1992, he hung the plaque in his courtroom and began a habit of opening his court sessions in prayer.

The American Civil Liberties Union (ACLU) and the Alabama Freethought Association sued, claiming that the prayers and plaque were violations of the Alabama and U.S. Constitutions. Initially, a judge in Montgomery ruled that Moore could keep the plaque but would have to stop the prayers. When, in January 1998, the Alabama Supreme Court threw the case out, ruling that the parties who had brought suit had no standing to do so since they had no legal disagreement with the judge, a spokesman for the ACLU publicly announced a desire for someone "who is affected by Moore's religious practices to file a lawsuit."[4]

Similarly, the ACLU in Columbus, Ohio, requested that a federal court stop the state from inscribing the state motto, which was adopted in 1959, on the Ohio statehouse. The offensive motto? "With God all things are possible." The ACLU's lawyers contended that the quote would "offend members of minority religions, and would be an unconstitutional promotion of religion."[5]

The courts aren't the only tool used to pursue and punish unpopular religious views. A recent study conducted by Bruce Bates, former publications director of the National Religious Broadcasters, revealed that religious radio and television broadcasters are seven times more likely than their secular counterparts to be audited by the Internal Revenue Service. Bates says that he believes the executive branch "has been using the IRS to go after . . . certain religious organizations and their leadership."[6]

Nor do such attacks occur only in the United States. In 1992, officers of the Canadian government seized transmitting equipment from several twenty-four-hour Christian television stations, one of which was operated by a church in Medicine Hat, Alberta. The reason for the government's action? The stations were operating illegally. This much was true, technically speaking. The stations were operating without licenses because it was impossible for an all-Christian television station to receive an operating permit from the Canadian Radio/Television and Telecommunications Commission (CRT). The CRT allowed all-rock music stations, all-sports stations, all-movie stations, but no all-Christian stations. It took a lawsuit to persuade the CRT to issue licenses to Christian broadcasters. When, on October 14, 1994, the CRT reversed its position, Gerard Renald Guay of the Canadian Center for Law and Justice exulted, "We rejoice that for the first time in close to seventy years, Christian stations will be authorized to operate in Canada."[7]

That case ended happily. Many others do not, such as the Colorado case that prohibited a teacher from leaving on his desk the Bible he had read earlier during a free period.[8] Another recent incident occurred in the U.S. Capitol building when a group of tourists paused to pray and were interrupted and warned that any noticeable prayer would be considered a "demonstration" that would result in ejection from the building and up to five hundred dollars in fines and six months in jail.[9]

If you or your children have not encountered such antagonism already, you may count yourself fortunate. But be prepared; the enforcers of the new tolerance will not let your Christian beliefs, behavior, lifestyle, and truth claims go unchallenged for long.

So what should you do? How can you respond with Christlike love?

- First, keep in mind that Christians seem to be most effective in engaging the government on issues of church and state, life and death, and marriage and family at the local level. I believe that is partly because we are most effective when we are *in relationship* with both our allies and our opponents. Consequently, it is crucial *at all levels* to build strong relationships—with school-board members, city-council members, county commissioners, state representatives, members of Congress, and especially those politicians or activists who oppose us. I am convinced that if the government leaders and political activists in our communities and nations knew more Christians—and were themselves known by Christians—it would have a profound effect not only for this present age but for the age to come.

  Take, for example, the experience of Tom Minnery, vice president of public policy for Focus on the Family. Tom was participating in a panel discussion at a University of Colorado conference when a woman stood in the audience and identified herself as a leader of a national gay and lesbian organization. Her next words surprised Tom:

  > She said that just prior to the conference she had visited [Focus on the Family headquarters]. She said she had sensed genuine love from our staff during her visit, and that she appreciated our work. . . . She displayed none of the anger that I often encounter at events like these. *Having met our people,* she seemed

to have a hard time seeing us as "the enemy"—or believing that's how we saw her. [italics added][10]

That's the idea. As we cultivate good relationships—especially with those who disagree with us—it
may become easier to scale the walls that divide us.

• If we say we are Christians and believe God's Word, then
we need to be obedient to 1 Timothy 2:1-2, which ad-
monishes us to pray "for kings and all those in authority, that we may live peaceful and quiet lives in all
godliness and holiness." It is much easier to act lovingly
toward someone for whom you've been praying.

• I believe we need to be as "wise as serpents and harmless
as doves," (Matthew 10:16, NKJV), learning all we can
about the political environment we live in so that we can
"understand the times," while at the same time learning
all we can about God's standards as laid out in the Bible.
How can we be good citizens of this world or of heaven
if we are not wise enough to know what either expects of
us? My experience leads me to conclude that the majority of Christians who are so adamant about having the
Ten Commandments taught in the classroom cannot
even recite what those commandments are. That is certainly not wisdom!

• Choose your issues wisely. There may seem to be hundreds of things happening in your school and community that make you mad or offend your principles. But
you can't speak out on every issue; you would soon ex-
haust yourself and your resources. You would also
probably gain a reputation that could cripple your future effectiveness. Speak out or stand up to a frontal as-

sault on your faith or a clear violation of moral decency, but don't think that you must protest *everything* that doesn't support the cause of Christ.

- Build a coalition. There is influence in numbers. Find other people who agree with you, and network with them. Agree together on the issues that must be addressed, and then pursue a solution with calm, careful logic. A coalition of men and women concerned about the moral and ethical well-being of a community can be a powerful force for good.

- Know the "whys" behind the issues you support or oppose. When you choose an issue and have a solid coalition behind you, be sure you are prepared to answer questions about why a particular stand is wrong—and what will make it right. The Bible instructs us to "sanctify Christ as Lord in your hearts, always being ready to make a defense to everyone who asks you to give an account for the hope that is in you, yet with gentleness and reverence" (1 Peter 3:15, NASB).

I suggest two levels of preparation: (1) be prepared to offer a moral and ethical defense for your position; and (2) give inward attention to your spiritual convictions. Because we live in a pluralistic society, you may be more effective in rebuilding community values by promoting the values vigorously and presenting your faith gently. Appeal to basic decency and the violation of common sense rather than appealing to biblical or church doctrine when making your case to a school or government body. This doesn't mean people should not eventually understand that the principles for which you stand are based on the character of God and the Lordship of Christ; it means that we should obey the biblical instruction to "let your speech always be gracious, seasoned with salt, so that you may know how you ought to answer every one" (Colossians 4:6, RSV).

Life and Death

The second key flash point in which the new tolerance rears its head in government today is in matters involving life and death. Now, according to the new tolerance, people may believe or claim anything. The only exceptions, of course, are those whose claims challenge the postmodern assertion that all truth claims are equal. And it is just here, in matters of life and death, where any government dominated by the new tolerance must quell Christian dissent.

For example, civil disobedience and peaceful protest have been distinctives of the political process in the U.S. since the days of Washington and Jefferson. They still are. In the course of a single daily news cycle, one may hear or read about a peaceful AIDS vigil conducted on the steps of a statehouse, fur protestors picketing a department store, students protesting a university's termination of affirmative-action preferences in admissions and financial-aid policy, movie stars blocking bulldozers with their bodies in an effort to save the environment, even illegal aliens demonstrating against policies that affect them. Such protestors are sometimes arrested. Sometimes they are prosecuted, even fined. But by far the stiffest penalties are reserved for those who dare to interrupt the abortion industry's "machinery of death."[11]

In 1989 the Feminist Women's Health Center sued five pro-life demonstrators for blocking the entrance to its Sacramento clinic and charged that the protestors had harassed patients and staff members. In 1991 Sacramento Superior Court

Judge James Long ordered the five demonstrators to pay the clinic's legal fees, amounting to nearly $100,000. In 1993 the state court of appeals upheld the decision. When the state supreme court refused to hear the case, the defendants appealed to the U.S. Supreme Court, arguing that the $100,000 award effectively penalized the protestors for exercising their First Amendment rights, since there was no evidence they had been violent. Without comment, the court let the penalty stand.[12]

In the same season, the Supreme Court rejected a free-speech appeal by sixteen abortion protestors who had been arrested for parading too close to the home of an abortion doctor, refused to hear a sweeping challenge to the severe limits that have been placed on abortion-clinic protests, and turned down appeals by pro-life protestors who were prosecuted as *racketeers* under the RICO statute, a 1970 law aimed at organized crime.

Why do the courts consistently subject abortion protestors to limits and penalties that are not applied to others? Because the opponents of abortion represent a challenge to the new tolerance, the doctrine that is spreading throughout the judicial, legislative, and executive branches of government. Those who oppose abortion do so not only because they believe abortion would be wrong "for them"; they assert that killing babies in or out of the womb (or "partially" born, as in "partial-birth abortion") is categorically wrong. And because the basic premise of their opposition is irreconcilable with the new tolerance, many in government (and not only the U.S. government) view them differently from those who protest the killing of baby seals or the cutting down of redwood trees. This explains why Pope John Paul II angered so many in France's government by visiting the grave of a longtime friend, pro-life geneticist Jerome Lejeune, who died in 1994. Socialist Party leaders denounced the

Pope's action, claiming that it might encourage abortion opponents, who bear "the mark of *intolerance*."[13]

The same kind of treatment awaits those who try to promote biblical perspectives on other issues of life and death, such as assisted suicide and euthanasia. For example, the hospice movement, an alternative to assisted suicide and euthanasia that focuses on providing comfort and care for the terminally ill, has recently come under attack. Government auditors have begun targeting hospice benefits, which are available when a doctor certifies that a patient has six months or less to live. Though 85 to 90 percent of patients do die within that period,[14] that is apparently not good enough for the U.S. Department of Health and Human Services, which launched Operation Restore Trust to investigate suspected fraud in the industry. Though the effort may have uncovered many instances of fraud, some in the industry felt targeted not because their practices are fraudulent but because they apparently value the preservation of life too highly.

Hospice nurse Michele Evans, writing in the *Los Angeles Times,* asked, "What message does it give when [Jack Kevorkian, who had, by early 1998, helped at least seventy-six people[15] commit suicide] gets front-page news on a regular basis," while hospices receive coverage "only when the government decides we're letting people live too long?"[16]

The message, if I might be so bold as to offer an answer, is that the new tolerance has become the order of the day.

So, what does the "more excellent way" of Christlike love look like in such matters of life and death?

- Remember to *aggressively* live in love while *humbly* pointing to the truth. Unfortunately, many women

choose abortion because it is a non-Christian who cries
with them when they receive the news of an unwelcome
pregnancy or because the Christians who are around
minister condemnation instead of forgiveness and reconciliation. Too many suffering patients choose assisted
suicide because they lack the comfort and support of
concerned Christians. Your effectiveness in pointing to
the truth will rise as your activity in such things as
crisis-pregnancy counseling and hospice increases.

• Try to keep in mind that ultimately it's not you the proponents of the new tolerance must argue with; it is the truth. It
is not you they reject; it is the Truth, Jesus himself. The opponents of truth should not be the objects of your hate or
scorn; you should instead be "sympathetic, brotherly, kindhearted, and humble in spirit" (1 Peter 3:8, NASB) toward
them, knowing that "they perish . . . because they refused to
love the truth and so be saved" (2 Thessalonians 2:10).

• Never forget the intense needs of those on all sides of the
issue. The unborn baby is a human being created in
God's image, a precious soul whom God loves; so is the
mother who may be considering taking that life. Be careful to treat both with Christlike love, doing all you can
to protect the life of the baby while addressing the needs
of the mother—sacrificially, if necessary. For example,
give your time as a childbirth coach, pledge your financial help to buy baby clothes, offer your support in ar-
ranging adoption, etc. Similarly, don't discount the
suffering of the terminally ill patient who cries out for
relief, or answer such pain with platitudes. Instead, support compassionate alternatives to euthanasia and assisted suicide with your time, effort, and contributions.

Marriage and Sexuality

The third flash point for biblically minded Christians in an age when government is dominated by the new tolerance is in matters involving marriage and sexuality. Just a few examples will illustrate how government and the new tolerance mix in this area.

Two bills were approved on July 15, 1997, by California's Senate Judiciary Committee. AB 257 declared homosexuality to be an official "civil right" on an equal level with race and nationality. It also inserted the words *sexual orientation* into the Fair Employment and Housing Act (FEHA). AB 310 went even further, allowing authorities to investigate and prosecute "churches, religious schools, missions, and all other religious corporations that discriminate." The bill also permitted FEHA investigators to audit the rental records of property owners and personnel records of employers—including churches—"to see if they have ever discriminated." These investigations would not require a search warrant, just cause, or even a complaint on file. "Gay activists could apply for work at churches and sue for discrimination when turned down," said Art Croney, executive director of the Sacramento-based Committee on Moral Concerns.[17]

In late 1996, the U.S. Postal Service's law-enforcement division issued a code of conduct forbidding its 4,600 inspectors and police officers from discriminating against homosexuals, even during off-duty hours. The new code required employees to sign a statement agreeing to follow the code. One employee refused to sign because he said he believes that homosexuality is a sin. Another wouldn't sign because he was afraid it would keep him from voicing his opinion against same-sex unions or homosexual pastors at his church.

The antidiscrimination clause of this code of conduct declared:

> Employees acting in an official capacity will not directly or indirectly authorize, permit or participate in discrimination based on age, gender, ethnic origin, physical or mental disability or sexual orientation against anyone, whether or not they are employees. Because we are a law enforcement agency, off-duty conduct that demonstrates an inability to be fair, objective and unbiased in dealings with others will not be tolerated.[18]

Although all cabinet-level departments except the Pentagon already have rules barring discrimination based on sexual orientation, the Postal Service code is *the only policy that extends to employees' off-duty hours.* Robert Maginnis, an analyst at the Family Research Council, warns that this policy sends the message that "people who have deeply held moral beliefs . . . need not apply for the federal jobs. . . . This is reverse discrimination of the worst kind."[19]

Such discrimination—and, increasingly, persecution—of those who hold biblical convictions in matters affecting marriage and sexuality will be the order of the day in a system of government dominated by adherents of the new tolerance.

All these things seem to confirm Philip Yancey's words of warning:

> Every year the church in the United States draws closer and closer to the situation faced by the New Testament church: an embattled minority living in a pluralistic, pagan society. Christians in places like Sri Lanka, Tibet, Sudan, and Saudi Arabia have faced open hostility from

their governments for years. But in the United States, with a history so congenial to the faith, we don't like it. [And we wonder,] What should we do about it?[20]

How *do* we respond in a Christlike manner to governmental policy that undermines biblical standards of marriage and sexuality and, in some cases, prosecutes those who hold such standards? It is impossible, of course, to prescribe specific responses for every imaginable circumstance in which government assails us or our faith. Still, the following are just a few examples of responses that may be helpful:

- Do not answer arrogance with arrogance. Too often, we Christians (perhaps because we know the truth that brings freedom[21]) tend to point out the sins and shortcomings of others rather boldly, without the slightest acknowledgment of our own imperfections. It is a constant but worthwhile challenge to cultivate the habit of humility that says, "You know, I'm a sinner too, and I don't have it all together, but let me say . . ."

- Counter principles, not people. It *is* people, of course, who advance wrong thinking and behavior. But to be effective, you must attack immoral principles, not people. Stick to the issues; stand firmly for principles, but resist the temptation to attack your opponents.

  Just before the apostle Peter admonished Christians to always be "ready to make a defense" (1 Peter 3:15, NASB), he commanded us to "be harmonious, sympathetic, brotherly, kindhearted, and humble in spirit; not returning evil for evil, or insult for insult, but giving a blessing instead" (1 Peter 3:8-9, NASB). And just following his endorsement of a ready defense, he advised, "Keep a good conscience so that in the thing in which you are slandered, those who revile your good behavior in Christ may be put to shame" (1 Peter 3:16, NASB).

- Defend the God-ordained institution of marriage between a man and a woman not only as biblical (Genesis 2:24) but also as foundational to the fabric of society and demonstrably crucial for the optimal health and development of children. This will mean compassionate opposition not only to homosexual unions but also to bigamy, polygamy, and divorce.

- In this, as in any area, be alert to counter "Doublethink" (the notion that contradictory ideas can all be true) and "Newspeak" (the false equations of new tolerance, such as "who I am equals what I do" and "nonagreement equals phobia," etc.) when you hear them. Don't allow those who disagree with you to label *your* disagreement as discrimination or phobia; kindly but firmly resist their labeling tactics.

- Look for opportunities to distinguish between homosexuals and homosexual behavior, between gays and the gay agenda. Take pains to communicate loving acceptance of the former even as you differ with the latter.

- Fight fire with . . . love. The natural tendency, of course, is to fight fire with fire. But remember, the true antidote to the new tolerance is authentic Christian love. Follow the creative example of the Christians in Ypsilanti, Michigan. When a local printer gently refused to print material promoting the homosexual agenda, homosexual activists reacted angrily and planned a demonstration in front of the printer's shop. On the day of the demonstration, police and news crews lined the streets, anticipating violence. Then a wonderful thing happened. About 150 Christians began arriving . . . "bearing more than a thousand cookies and gallons of hot coffee and cold punch that they intended to offer to the homosexual demonstrators."[22] When fewer than ten homosexual activists showed up, they were welcomed by the Christians who showered them with refreshments and conversation. The potentially explosive situation was defused by an outpouring of Christian love.

Chapter 9

TOLERANCE AND SOCIETY

When the smokestacks at the paper mill first began churning their waste into the air over the small Midwestern town, the residents complained. The fine dust blanketed everything, they said, and the acrid smell was everywhere. It seeped into the upholstery of their cars and crept into their homes. It seemed to flavor their food and water. It settled into the fibers of their clothing. It penetrated the very pores of their skin.

But the odor was the smell of money, the town fathers told them repeatedly. The offensive stench meant jobs for their sons and husbands. It promised prosperity and security.

"And besides," they said, "you'll get used to it."

And they did. After a couple weeks, the smell was no longer sickening. In a few months, the residents didn't even notice it. A year or two later, the town's citizens thought of the horrible odor only when visitors to the town commented on it. The odorous output of the mill had become so pervasive, it had become unremarkable to those who were most affected by it day after day.

The fate of that town is a parable of the ideas that have come to permeate our society and impress themselves upon us from all sides. The new tolerance unrelentingly inserts itself subtly into our lives, via television images and song lyrics. Whether you know it or not, the deceptive doctrine of the new tolerance—and the accompanying idolatry it fosters—is all around you, seeping not only into your mind but into the minds of your children and other loved ones. And if we are not careful and alert, it will soon become unremarkable—and thus irresistible—to those who are most endangered by it.

DANGER ZONES

In this chapter, we will look at the influence of the new tolerance in four areas: art and literature, entertainment, health, and science. As we do so, we will seek to answer the biblical question, "If the foundations are destroyed, what can the righteous do?" (Psalm 11:3, NASB). What *can* we do? How can we respond to the pervasive influence of the new tolerance in society? And how can we protect our children from its dangers?

Art and Literature

Average citizens and parents in many Western countries have often found themselves shaking their heads in the past few decades at what many in society have come to view as art. Among the most bizarre examples are projects funded in the U.S. by the National Endowment for the Arts (NEA). The NEA's tax-funded "art" displays have included

- a young woman urinating in a toilet;
- a photograph of a crucifix in a jar of urine;
- a three-foot mound of excrement;

- a dismembered sculpture of two women involved in a sexual act.[1]

How could *anyone* label such exhibits "art," let alone spend public funds on them? Simple. Such displays are partly a result of the influence of the new tolerance.

Look at it this way: If all beliefs, behaviors, lifestyles, and truth claims are *equal*, then there is no standard one can use to say that the *Mona Lisa* is better art than a Robert Mapplethorpe photo of a homoerotic act. In fact, to even suggest that a painting or sculpture is a "masterpiece" is offensive, writes William A. Henry III, "because it implies that one idea, culture or human being can actually be better than another."[2] In a society dominated by the new tolerance, any objective definition of what art is becomes impossible; art becomes *whatever the artist—or audience—says it is.*

A similar dynamic is at work in the world of literature. Once upon a time, people understood when they read books or articles that they were reading the author's point of view. The author may have expressed himself poorly or well, but he determined what his words were intended to mean; the reader's job was to grasp the author's meaning.

Today, in our society at large, as in our schools and universities, that is often not true. As Jim Leffel explains:

> To postmodern thinkers, readers . . . aren't learners standing under the authority of the author and text. They are no longer on a quest to discover what the author and the words of the text mean. Instead, readers are elevated to the status of authority over the text. . . . The intent of the author becomes irrelevant. . . . At the same time, though,

even the reader isn't an authority in any objective or final
sense. *All readings are equally valid,* and all readers are
their own authorities. [italics added][3]

In other words, in today's society, you may read *The Diary of
Anne Frank* and view it as the diary of a Jewish girl hiding from
the Nazis in the midst of the Holocaust. If I read the same book
and conclude that it's an auto-maintenance manual, *I would be
right . . . and so would you!* Because according to the new tolerance, what Anne Frank intended to record or communicate is ir-
relevant; the book means whatever I say it means and whatever
you say it means. Our claims, our beliefs, are *equally valid.*

This is best illustrated, perhaps, by the recent release of an
"inclusive" version of the Bible by Oxford University Press.
Kenneth Woodward, the religion editor of *Newsweek* magazine,
comments:

> Readers who find the Bible sexist, racist, elitist and insen-
> sitive to the physically challenged, take heart. Oxford Uni-
> versity Press's new "inclusive language version" of the
> New Testament and Psalms has cleaned up God's act. In
> this version, God is no longer "Father" and Jesus is no
> longer "Son." The hierarchical title of "Lord" is excised as
> an archaic way to address God. Nor does God (male pro-
> nouns for the deity have been abolished) rule a "king-
> dom"; as the editors explain, the word has a "blatantly
> androcentric and patriarchal character." . . . Even God's
> metaphorical "right hand" has been amputated out of def-
> erence to the lefthanded. Some examples:
>
> • In the majestic opening of John's Gospel, "the glory he
>   has from the Father as the only Son of the Father" be-

comes "the glory as of a parent's only child." (John 1:14)

- The Lord's Prayer now begins like this: "Father-Mother, hallowed be your name. May your dominion come." (Luke 11:2)

- Jesus's own self-understanding as God's only son is generalized to: "No one knows the Child except the Father-Mother; and no one knows the Father-Mother except the Child . . ." (Matthew 11:27)

- Avoiding another traditional phrase, "Son of Man," the Oxford text reads: "Then they will see the Human One coming in clouds with great power and glory." (Mark 13:26)

The editors do not claim that Jesus spoke in gender-neutral language. But they obviously think he should have. The changes they have made are not merely cosmetic. They represent a fundamental reinterpretation of what the New Testament says—and how it says it.[4]

In the thrall of the new tolerance, there is nothing wrong in the slightest with changing the words of the Bible because the Bible—like any "work of literature"—has no objective meaning at all. It only means what each individual reader says it means.

So what's a concerned Christian to do? How can we respond to the new tolerance as it manifests itself in art and literature? The following might suggest some starting points:

- Reinforce the concept that true art (whether visual, musical, or literary) is that which reflects or reinforces "whatever is true, whatever is noble, whatever is right, whatever is pure, whatever is lovely, whatever is admirable . . . excellent or praiseworthy" (Philippians 4:8). Art, then, should reflect and glorify (even peripherally, perhaps) the nature of God; anti-art accomplishes the opposite, and non-art does neither.

- If you encounter the suggestion that books (or movies or works of art) mean whatever the listener, reader, or viewer says they mean, gently and tactfully point out the irony in such a statement. For example, a friend of mine, who is a professor at a secular university, says he has responded to such concepts by smiling warmly and saying, "So, what I hear you saying is that Jesus Christ is Lord!" The only way for his listeners to argue consistently is to admit that his statement is true; if they disagree with his interpretation, they admit that they intended their words to be understood objectively, thus contradicting their own argument.

- Help your children understand, as early as possible, that *words have meaning.* The meaning may sometimes be poorly phrased or misunderstood, but if they were devoid of meaning, there would be *no point* in writing or talking! This may have been an obvious point to previous generations, but that is no longer true.

- Don't fall for the lie that says that since we cannot know *everything* a writer (or artist) intended to communicate, we cannot know *anything* about what he or she meant. This is a fallacy author Dennis McCallum refutes specifically in relation to the Bible:

> God has chosen language as his primary medium of revelation, and we believe that we can accurately understand the intent of God's revelation to a *substan-*

tial degree. The mission of hermeneutics—the science of interpretation—is to adjust our understanding based on cultural and language differences at the time of writing, so we may know the author's intended meaning. This mission has been largely successful.[5]

Entertainment

The rumors had swirled since the show's debut in 1994. Then, when news leaked that the star of the show wanted her character to discover that she was homosexual, the rumors fueled a media frenzy. By April 1997, when Ellen Degeneres's namesake character on her sitcom, *Ellen,* unintentionally confessed her homosexuality over an airport PA system, the story was front-page news, earning the actress a spate of talk-show appearances and newsmagazine covers.

The excitement, of course, was due to the "history-making" nature of the decision. Ellen would be the first openly gay star of a television show. In retrospect, perhaps, the move is far less shocking and revolutionary than it appeared at the time. After all, from the days of the seventies sitcom *Soap,* television has been central to the drive, fueled by the new tolerance, to gain approval for and participation in the homosexual lifestyle—a drive that has been so successful that as of February 1997 (before Ellen's "coming out") twenty-two homosexual characters populated the television airwaves, from *The Simpsons* to *Melrose Place.*[6]

Why such overrepresentation of homosexuals on television (and in movies)? The words of Judge Robert Bork suggest one possibility:

Hollywood's writers, producers, and executives think popular entertainment affects behavior. It is not merely that they sell billions of dollars of advertising on television on the premise that they can influence behavior; they also think that the content of their programs can reform society.... They understand that no single program will change attitudes much, but they rely upon the cumulative impact of years of television indoctrination.[7]

It's not just homosexuality that today's entertainment industry promotes in an effort (though not, we should reiterate, a human conspiracy; see chapter 5) to "reform society." The producers, writers, and performers in the fields of television, film, and music give assent—and impetus—to the ideas and ideals of the new tolerance.

Oliver Stone's movies *JFK* and *Nixon* are typical of the doctrine of the new tolerance operating in society. Stone apparently felt little allegiance to facts in his portrayals of Kennedy's assassination and Nixon's downfall because *facts are not the point* in a society dominated by the new tolerance. Stone's vision of "history" is *no less valid* than historians who may have spent a lifetime chronicling facts.

Even the wholesome Disney tradition has become saturated with the new tolerance. The animated feature *The Lion King* is a mesmerizing story that incorporates elements of monism,[8] pantheism,[9] and sorcery with its theme, "The Circle of Life." *Pocahontas* tells the revisionist tale of a noble Indian princess who falls in love with a White male (representative of a corrupt, oppressive culture).

Take, for example, the pantheism evident in the hit song from *Pocahontas,* "Colors of the Wind":

You think you own whatever land you land on;
the earth is just a dead thing you can claim;
but I know ev'ry rock and tree and creature
has a life, has a spirit, has a name.[10]

You or your children would probably recognize and reject such pantheistic philosophy if it were presented directly, wouldn't you? But when it is presented in the lyrics of a song, sung by an animated character on the silver screen? In such a way, as Professor David Wells says, "Film and television now provide the sorts of values that were once provided by the family."[11] The dangerous doctrine of the new tolerance is being slyly inserted into your mind, your children's minds, and into the society that surrounds you. But it is possible to counter the dangers of the new tolerance in ways such as the following:

- First, parents, remember: *You* are in charge of raising your children, not Hollywood, not Madison Avenue, and not the toy companies. No matter how much your children may object, it is your responsibility to say no to toys, music, movies, or other forms of entertainment that undermine or compromise Christian concepts and standards. One father I know agreed with his teenage son that the boy could buy any music cassette or CD without a parental-advisory sticker, provided Dad listened to it (or read the lyrics sheet) before the son listened to it. If Dad approved not only of the language but of the more subtle messages in the music, fine; if not, they would return the cassette or CD to the store. On one occasion, father and son returned *three music cas-*

settes in less than an hour to a mall music store in one afternoon before finding a selection that was acceptable! The dad would always explain his decisions to his son, and while the boy was not always pleased, he soon learned to filter media messages on his own.

• Don't complain about the problem; contribute to the solution. A friend of mine works in Hollywood. I once sat across the table from him, carrying on about all that was wrong in movies and television. He stopped me cold.

"Just once," he said, nearly shaking his finger at me, "I wish the Christians who don't like what they see coming out of Hollywood would actually *do* something about it." I was surprised at his words but even more surprised at the pain and the weariness that showed on his face. "Where are all the other Christian screenwriters and producers and directors? They're not in Hollywood, I can tell you that, because most of the time I feel all alone as a Christian in this industry." His voice softened then. "If you want to work in a real mission field," he said, "come to Hollywood."

His words silenced me. His point was well taken. Our society will not be helped by complaining; what it needs is Christians who are willing to enter into relationship with Christians *and* non-Christians who are influenced by the new tolerance that pervades our society.

• Learn critical reading, viewing, and listening . . . and teach it to your children. Learn to

Understand: What is the book/show/song saying?

Evaluate: How is the message being presented? Are any biases evident? Are all sides being shown? Is the author's/reporter's/performer's agenda evident . . . or hidden? How does the message compare with the truth of Scripture and the revelation of God in Christ?

Respond: Does my evaluation require me to accept or reject the message?

- Help your children critically evaluate the media messages that bombard them constantly. Watch television *with* your children. Pause the videotape of *Pocahontas* to ask what the movie is really communicating. When commercials interrupt their favorite sitcom, help them to *understand, evaluate,* and *respond* to what they are watching.

- Take every opportunity to use society's own messengers to communicate biblical messages. For example, the pseudospiritual lyrics of many popular songs offer a great opportunity to present biblical answers to spiritual questions. One teenager I know will occasionally answer the plaintive plea of the song, "Who Will Save Your Soul?" by saying, "I know who saves my soul; do you?" Another has used Joan Osborne's question, "What If God Was One of Us?" to introduce his friends to the gospel message by reading Philippians 2:5-11 from his pocket New Testament. And though Fiona Apple may not be singing of God when she testifies, "I need to be redeemed to the one I've sinned against" (in her song "Criminal"), an alert Christian can use that line as a springboard to witnessing to the truth that we've all sinned against God and that there is a Redeemer (Romans 3:23-26).

Health and Medicine

He's been on the cover of *Time* magazine. He has appeared on nearly every morning talk show and evening newsmagazine. His books soar to the top of the best-seller lists. A popular audio CD of music and meditations bears his name, and his Web site routinely records over a million "hits" a month.

He's Dr. Andrew Weil, author of *Spontaneous Healing* and *8 Weeks to Optimum Health*. And he is one of the most successful practitioners of "alternative medicine" and "New Age remedies," along with Deepak Chopra (*Ageless Body, Timeless Mind*), Marianne Williamson (*The Healing of America*), and Bernie Siegel (*Peace, Love and Healing*).

These practitioners and their "therapies" are rapidly gaining popularity and acceptance, making alternative health care a $14 billion industry. And some of their ideas are not so unusual: eat less fat, they say; exercise regularly, and cut down on stress. But they don't stop there. Chopra, for example, is a practitioner of Ayurvedic medicine, the traditional medicine of India, which not only involves a balanced diet and herbal supplements but also incorporates Hindu teachings (such as the concept of *Prana,* the "life energy" that flows through all of us) and practices (such as *yagyas,* religious ceremonies that solicit help from Hindu gods).

In addition, much as transcendental meditation (TM) popularized Hindu practices in the seventies, so another practice, "Therapeutic Touch," has spread Eastern mysticism through the halls of science and medicine:

According to [Dolores Krieger, one of the "experts" in the "Therapeutic Touch" movement], "Therapeutic Touch is a healing practice based on the conscious use of the hands to direct or modulate, for therapeutic purposes, selected nonphysical human energies that activate the physical body."

In practice, a healer must become "centered" before attempting Therapeutic Touch. Centering is "an act of self-searching, a going within to explore the deeper levels of yourself."[12]

The alternative therapies championed by Weil, Chopra, Krieger, and others include hypnotism, meditation and "channeling," cranial manipulation, and "psychic healing," among others. Many of these "healing" methods employ the techniques and terminology of Eastern religions, referring to "spiritual orientation"[13] and connecting with "a Higher Power."[14] But few of them are supported by empirical evidence. The complaint of Dr. Arnold Relman, former editor of the *New England Journal of Medicine* and professor emeritus at Harvard Medical School, about Andrew Weil's methodology is often echoed regarding others: "Weil wants you to believe that you don't need the scientific approach, that you don't need to demand evidence. . . . I resent well-educated people exploiting irrational elements in our culture, and that's what he's doing."[15]

Dr. Relman's frustration is understandable because "alternative medicine" has arisen and prospers largely as a result of the new tolerance and its stepchild, multiculturalism. Dr. Donal O'Mathuna, writing in *The Death of Truth,* points out that the proponents and practitioners of many alternative medicines not only *exploit* irrational elements in our culture, they *rely* on them:

Alternative medicine apologists use the postmodern method to establish the acceptability of their view. To be specific, they use three postmodern arguments:

1. They cast doubt on the findings of biochemical medicine, arguing that it is merely an outgrowth of a

Western (modernist) mentality, which is materialistic, male-dominated, and cold.

2. They argue that alternative medicine is the product of the "marginalized" or oppressed minority culture in the West. They claim that criticisms of alternative medicine are nothing but power posturing by the medical establishment, which endeavors to preserve its control over medicine.

3. They seek to replace objective, rational, experimental data as the basis for accepting the value of a therapy with a new basis: personal experience.[16]

No one doubts that the medical community still has much to learn, and there are certainly forms of treatment waiting to be discovered. But much alternative medicine is dangerous. It is dangerous not only because it mixes commonsense health care with Eastern spiritualism, thus introducing many doctors, nurses, students, and patients—perhaps even you or your children—to idolatry disguised as medicine; it also poses dangers to those who need proven, reliable treatment. A victim of liver disease who rejects conventional treatment for the herbal healing properties of milk thistle may be helped; he or she may also be immeasurably harmed . . . in the name of the new tolerance.

But, while the new tolerance may be more subtle, more cleverly disguised, in health and medicine, it is still possible not only to recognize but also to counter its insidious influence. For example:

- Be alert for key words or phrases in discussions of health and medicine, such as *centered, channeling, Higher Power, spiritual,* and *psychic,* that may indicate the presence of Eastern philosophy and religion. You needn't categorically reject all "alternative" forms of medicine (such as herbal remedies, stress-reduction techniques, etc.), but don't accept idolatry or occultic practices disguised as medicine.

- Don't be afraid to ask questions (and teach your children to do the same). If your doctor or healthcare practitioner advises techniques or procedures that are unfamiliar to you, ask for documentation of the method's effectiveness (not just anecdotal evidence), and don't hesitate to insist upon a second opinion.

- Be wary of the politics of power at work in conventional medicine *and* alternative medicine. A treatment should not be considered worthwhile simply because it is Eastern rather than Western methodology or because it is an example of "female-dominated nursing" instead of male-dominated "medical imperialism," but because it is supported by verifiable data according to the most reliable procedures available.

- Insist that religious content in medicine be acknowledged as such, not because religion is necessarily incompatible with science (it's not), but because medicine should not be used as an enlistment tool for Eastern religions.[17]

- Don't be fooled into thinking that medical quackery disappeared with snake oil. One survey found that 26.6 percent of Americans had used a questionable health-care treatment.[18] In the age of the new tolerance, perhaps more than ever, let the buyer beware.

Science

Not only has the new tolerance transformed health care, entertainment, and the arts in our society; it has also affected the study and practice of the sciences.

For example, a few years ago, Professor David Ayres of Dallas Baptist University presented evidence that some of the differences between men and women originate in biology and genetics. His research, however, inflamed campus feminists, who presumably prefer to believe the feminist dogma (regardless of *any* evidence to the contrary, scientific or otherwise) that there are no differences between the two sexes other than those imposed by culture and environment.

The university's administration, intimidated by the feminists, leveled charges against Professor Ayres and directed Dean John Jeffrey to investigate. Jeffrey refused; he maintained that Ayres was performing legitimate scholarly research and that his rights to due process were being infringed by the university's tactics. Both men were fired.[19]

Another scientist named Dean Kenyon, a prominent biologist on the faculty of San Francisco State University, recently confronted the effects of the new tolerance. Though he was once a true believer in Darwinism, Kenyon had for some time exposed his introductory students to what Chuck Colson calls "biology's trade secret: that the standard Darwinian model of evolution is riddled with problems."[20]

Kenyon was not teaching Creationism; he was not even advocating disbelief in evolution. He was simply pointing out the disturbing pattern of difficulties in Darwinian theory. Apparently, however, this was too much for the "scientists" at the university. They accused him of teaching religion and removed him from the

classroom. When this didn't work (the school's Academic Freedom Committee and other groups quickly defended Kenyon's
academic freedom), Kenyon's colleagues tried another tactic.

In the words of Chuck Colson, the university's biology department met and "voted 27 to 5 that naturalistic evolution is
the only theory admissible in biology—and that reference to an
intelligent cause at the origin of life is strictly unscientific."[21]

Colson goes on to exclaim, "What a caricature of real science. With this resolution, quips science writer Paul Nelson, we
have witnessed nothing less than the birth of a new method in
science. Why run costly experiments? To do science today, all
we need is a pen and a sheet of paper."[22]

That may seem like an oversimplification, but the point of
science in the age of the new tolerance (as in medicine and history) is not *facts* but *power*. And not only power but also experience. Lee Campbell, chair of the Division of Natural Sciences at
Ohio Dominican College, points out a growing affinity between
science and mysticism:

> Mystical scientists view traditional science negatively. . . .
> [They] believe a more enlightened science is possible.
> Enlightened science, as usually defined, is "inclusive,"
> "holistic," and nurturing of life.[23]

Campbell goes on to quote Fritjof Capra, "the best-selling
apologist for postmodern mystical science," from Capra's book
The Tao of Physics:

> This book aims at improving the image of science by
> showing that there is an essential harmony between the
> spirit of Eastern wisdom and Western science. It attempts
> to suggest that modern physics goes far beyond technol-

ogy, that the way—or Tao—of physics can be a path with a heart, a way to spiritual knowledge and self-realization.[24]

Is this science or religion? It is both. It is science in the thrall of the new tolerance, which simultaneously—and paradoxically—includes antipathy for "religion" (if the word means traditional Christian views of Creation, for example) while incorporating "spirituality" (though strictly of the Eastern, monistic, and pantheistic varieties). It is also a "science" that increasingly denies rationality and objectivity (the very pillars of scientific discovery) in favor of non-Western concepts, such as intuition and "self-realization."

But what can we do? We can't reasonably expect to counter the influence of so many in the scientific community, can we? We can't erase the damage that's been done, can we?

Perhaps not. But that's not the point. King David's words in Psalm 11:3 are as relevant today as they were when he first wrote them: "When the foundations are being destroyed, what can the righteous do?" If we read the rest of the psalm that follows his question, we discover the answer: When the foundations are being destroyed, *God is still on the throne.* What can the righteous do? *Go on being righteous.*

How do we do that? Let me suggest just a few starting points that relate to the influence of new tolerance on science:

- Recognize the relational and emotional needs that make the new tolerance so attractive to those who propagate it *and* to those who fall for it. Recognize also the relational and emotional needs that the new tolerance creates or aggravates, one of which is addressed by Dennis McCallum in *The Death of Truth:*

At its core, postmodern culture is profoundly lonely.
When people exchange the possibility of a servant-
style love for the hollow values of "respect" and "toleration," the result is interpersonal distance. They
become wrapped up in avoiding "off-limits" statements, avoiding disagreements with another's views,
and standing up for their own rights. Christians . . .
can build real relationships and community the secular world can only envy. Many postmodernists have
been won to Christ after they beheld a group of
Christians sharing the love of Christ with one another.[25]

Loneliness is certainly not the only result of the new
tolerance, nor is it the only motivation that prompts people to seek answers in the empty promises of the new tolerance. A craving for acceptance is probably a frequent
motivation, as is a desire for approval and respect. If we
can recognize the needs that motivate others' beliefs and
behavior, we can then go on to respond more effectively.

- Encourage Christians who work in the scientific field;
  help them deal with the loneliness and hopelessness that
  may arise in a field so heavily influenced by postmodernism and atheism.
- Don't be intimidated. You may feel ill-equipped, if you
  are a nonscientist, to discuss the influence of the new
  tolerance with those in the field. However, remember
  that scientists are people too, and they face the same
  moral, relational, and spiritual dilemmas you do.
- Keep in mind that postmodernism in science falls prey
  to the same error as it does in many other areas: internal

inconsistency. In other words, "they use observation and logical inference to reach the conclusion that observation and logical inference tell us nothing. They argue in a circle, only defeating themselves. By using the tools of science, they demonstrate that they too believe these tools work."[26]

Chapter 10

Tolerance and the Church

"Before repairing the ruins of our society," writes J. B. Cheaney, "Christians had better see to the crumbling walls of the church and reestablish the mandate we were given here. God is not here for us; we are here for him. When by his grace we do good, it is not for goodness' sake but for the praise of his glory. Our primary purpose is not to establish a moral society but to glorify God and pray that our faithfulness to him will be reflected in our culture."[1]

We have seen, in countless examples and in graphic detail, how the new tolerance has infused education, government, and society in general . . . much to the danger and detriment of us and our children. But the destructive doctrine of new tolerance has invaded the church as well. And what the adversary, our ancient foe, has failed to accomplish through fire and famine, he is already achieving with the cooperation of churches and churchgoers themselves—the marginalization and subversion of the church itself!

Consider the following statistics:

- Fifty-seven percent of *churched youth* do not believe an objective standard of truth exists;[2]

- Almost as many Bible-believing, conservative *Christian adults*—53 percent—do not believe in absolute truth;[3]
- Eighty-four percent of first-year *Christian college students* cannot intelligently defend or explain their beliefs;[4]
- Two-thirds of the 70 percent of Americans who say it is important to follow the teachings of the Bible *reject moral absolutes.*[5]

The barbarians are not only at the gate; as the comic-strip character Pogo famously observed, "We have met the enemy, and *he is us!*"

THE WHITE FLAG OF SURRENDER

The surrender of the Christian church to the ideas and ideals of the new tolerance has begun in earnest and is proceeding with frightening speed on three fronts: in leadership, in the seminaries, and in the pews themselves.

In January 1998, Bishop Frank Tracy Griswold was installed as the spiritual leader of 2.4 million Episcopalians, a denomination that is sharply divided over such issues as the ordination of practicing homosexuals. In his inaugural homily, the sixty-year-old Griswold said that the Anglican tradition possesses "a unique capacity for diversity" and declared that there are "different dimensions of truth."[6] Griswold's comments did not give encouragement to those who are praying and hoping for a revival of biblical faith and practice in his denomination.

A Canadian pastor friend of mine, Steve Brown, had the opportunity to hear the dean of a mainline divinity school speak to Steve's seminary apologetics class. The visiting professor told about his journey from evangelical apologetics professor to self-proclaimed atheist or (on "good days") agnostic. Steve writes:

> He also shared . . . his belief that *each culture develops [its] own reality or truth.* He stated that, just as Santa Claus doesn't need to be real to have an effect, so different religions or beliefs are equally real regardless of their foundation in truth or fact.
>
> As the time for questions began . . . I asked the visitor, "Do you believe there is absolute moral truth?" Although a long answer was given, the answer was "no," and he returned to his argument that *"each culture and even subculture determines [its] own reality or truth."*
>
> I then asked him, "If there is no absolute truth, does that mean that what Hitler did was right in his culture but wrong in our culture?" The dean said that I was correct. [italics added][7]

What a tragedy. Instead of teaching the truth of the Scriptures, that divinity-school dean was echoing the tenets of the new tolerance.

Such views are not only creeping into our pulpits and podiums, however; they are in the pews as well. Three researchers, writing in *Theology Today,* identified a growing phenomenon in one Christian denomination.[8] They document a prevailing attitude among baby boomers that is virtually indistinguishable from the new tolerance as it exists outside the church "in its stress on acceptance of differences, its tolerance of uncertainty, its strong commitment to individualism, and its . . . position on social and moral issues." These baby boomers, the researchers report,

. . . have come to terms with the multiple, often conflicting, cultural messages they receive in this world: they
accept that variety in truth claims is inevitable.

While they are clear about their own beliefs (as we
have seen, they tend to be conventional Christians), [they]
are reluctant to make claims of ultimate authority for
Christianity. Few would agree that salvation is only
through Jesus Christ or that Christ is the only source of
absolute truth. Rather, they maintain that other faith traditions are equal claimants to truth insights and that it
would be inappropriate for Christians to challenge those
alternative visions. . . . Many . . . go so far as to say that
they would be content if their children adopted non-
Western religions "as long as they are happy" and as long
as they are moral citizens.[9]

If such beliefs reflect the view from the pew, then the church
is in grave danger. In the words of Søren Kierkegaard, "As soon
as Christ's kingdom comes to terms with the world, Christianity
is abolished."[10]

Though such accommodation is indeed occurring in many
areas in the church today, it is most pronounced and most pervasive in three areas that pose a grave danger for us and for those
we love.

By the Book

Marcus J. Borg of Oregon State University is among the most
well-known Bible scholars today, particularly in the field of historical Jesus scholarship. He identifies himself as a Christian,
and his views are painfully common in parts of the church today. Of the Bible, he says:

I view the Bible as the response of one broad cultural stream to the experience of God. Its origin is not supernatural but human. . . . The truth of Christianity does not depend on the literal truth or historical infallibility of the Bible. To use a specific example, do we as Christians believe in the resurrection of Jesus because we have infallible accounts from eyewitnesses, in other words, because the Gospel stories of Easter "prove" that the resurrection really happened? Some Christians do, and I have heard Easter sermons like this. But . . . I would argue that the truth of Easter does not depend on whether there really was an empty tomb, or whether anything happened to the body of Jesus. The truth of Easter is that Jesus continued to be a living reality after his death. . . .[11]

Professor Borg, who was also a member of the infamous "Jesus Seminar,"[12] could hardly be considered an evangelical Christian. But the postmodern views he expresses are becoming disturbingly common in evangelical churches today, as the following story may illustrate:

The weekly Bible study began with comfortable predictability. After the customary pie, the members got cups of coffee and settled into their familiar niches around the room. Charlie, the leader, cleared his throat to signal that things were starting. As he did with merciless regularity each week, he began with the question, "Well, what do these verses mean to you?"

The discussion followed a familiar pattern. Each responded to what the verses meant to him or her, and the group reached its weekly general consensus—at least on the easier verses. They all knew what was coming, however; another stalemate between Donnell and Maria. Donnell had been a Christian for several years and was the self-appointed, resident theologian. For some reason he always seemed to lock horns with Maria, a relatively new Christian, yet an enthusiastic student of the Bible.

The scene repeated itself every time they came to difficult verses. The passage would elicit conflicting interpretations. Donnell would argue vehemently for the interpretation of his former pastor, which usually seemed a bit forced to the rest of the group. But it was Maria, being new and perhaps more straightforward, who would challenge Donnell. Because she didn't know the Bible that well yet, she would relate the difficult verse to her Christian experience in a way that contradicted Donnell's interpretation. Donnell would only redouble his efforts.

The stalemate usually ended with Charlie, the leader, or Betty, the resident peacemaker, bringing "resolution" to the discussion. One of them would calmly conclude by saying, "Well, this is another example of how reading the Bible is a matter of personal interpretation and how a verse can mean one thing to one person and something else to another." The group members would leave with a vague, hollow feeling in their chests.[13]

Professor Walt Russell, who wrote that account for his article, "What It Means to Me," which appeared in *Christianity Today,* points out that such approaches to Bible study—common in the church today—reflect the influence of postmodern ideas on the church. "The meaning of a text," he writes, "never changes. Our first goal [in Bible study] is to discover this fixed thing. In contrast, the *significance* of that text to me and others is very fluid and flexible. By confusing these two aspects of the interpretation process, we evangelicals approach the Bible with an interpretive relativism. If it means one thing to you and something contradictory to me, we have no ultimate court of appeals. . . . The reader allegedly 'creates meaning.'"[14]

Any approach to the Bible that allows each reader to decide for himself or herself what the text means, without "imposing" any outside ideas (even if they were God's ideas!) on anyone, may be "tolerant." It is also an approach that reduces the Bible to nothing more than a self-help manual and strips the Word of God of its authority and power, threatening the very foundations of the church—and of your faith.

So how can we respond? What can we do to counter this attack on the very Word of God?

- First, examine your own faith and practice. Do you regard the Bible as God's inspired Word? Do you *read* it? Do you study it? If we hope to stand for the integrity of God's Word in his church, *there is no substitute for a familiarity with and knowledge of the Bible* (Deuteronomy 6:6).
- Strive to differentiate, in personal and corporate Bible study, between the *meaning* of the text and the *significance,* or application, of the text. The question is not, "What does it mean *to me?*" but rather, "What does it mean?" and "How do I *apply it* to me?"
- Politely but firmly resist attempts to deconstruct the Word of God, approaching the text as though its meaning is *decided* rather than *discerned* by the reader or hearer (2 Timothy 2:15; 2 Peter 1:20). Consider studying

the basic rules of Bible interpretation as a defense against deconstructionism (R. C. Sproul's book *Knowing Scripture* is an excellent resource for this).

- Parents, do not delegate the Christian education of your children to the church. God commanded:

These commandments that I give you today are to be upon your hearts. Impress them on your children. Talk about them when you sit at home and when you walk along the road, when you lie down and when you get up. Tie them as symbols on your hands and bind them on your foreheads. Write them on the doorframes of your houses and on your gates. (Deuteronomy 6:6-9)

Teach your children to value and revere the Bible as God's Word. Teach them how to read it, study it, and apply it to their lives.

Love, Sex, and Marriage

Christian churches and denominations, both mainline and evangelical, have been gripped by a struggle for and against the new tolerance in the areas of love, sex, and marriage. Evangelicals' views of premarital sex and cohabitation have become more permissive, and while the church still takes a generally disapproving view of divorce (while commendably becoming more responsive to the victims of the tragedy), the response often avoids any mention of willful divorce as sin, concentrating instead on the practical ramifications of "broken families," a far more politically correct approach. But the most pronounced effects of the new tolerance on the church, as in other areas, may be seen in the church's approach to homosexual behavior, homosexual marriage, and the ordination of practicing homosexuals.

Two churches in North Carolina became the center of a 1992 controversy in the 15.2-million-member Southern Baptist Convention, America's largest Protestant denomination. Pullen Memorial Baptist Church, in Raleigh, blessed the union of two homosexual men; Binkley Memorial Baptist Church, in Chapel Hill, ordained an openly homosexual man as a minister. The incidents prompted a 1993 revision of the Southern Baptist Convention's constitution, giving the denomination power to oust congregations that condone homosexuality.

Reverend Mahan Siler, the pastor of Pullen Memorial Baptist Church, said he regretted that the denomination did not distinguish "between sexual behavior that's exploitative and sexual behavior that's in a caring, committed relationship. I think the church ought to support caring, committed relationships."[15]

Other denominations have faced similar struggles. The homosexual agenda has enjoyed growing acceptance in the Episcopal church and in the Presbyterian church (USA), forcing many Christians to face the difficult choice between leaving the denomination or staying in an attempt to reform the denomination from within.

Though the 8.5-million-member United Methodist Church (UMC) has officially reaffirmed the church's traditional teachings on sexuality and marriage, homosexual activists continue to gain ground. Pastor Jimmy Creech, of the 1,900-member First United Methodist Church in Omaha, Nebraska, conducted a lesbian wedding at the church (he was later suspended for sixty days with full pay and benefits). Princeton University's UMC chaplain Sue Ann Morrow performed a wedding ceremony in a campus chapel for two homosexuals who were also professing atheists and has stated publicly that she intends to continue to conduct same-sex weddings in the future. At last report, her bishop had taken no administrative action against her. And a new caucus group, CORNET (Covenant Relationships Network), is lobbying for same-sex marriage in the UMC, calling on churches and clergy to bless such unions as an "essential form of pastoral support."[16]

And while the Most Reverend George L. Carey, the spiritual leader of the seventy-million-member Anglican Church, recently cautioned against the ordination of homosexuals, he did not do so on biblical grounds. He stated that homosexuals should not be ordained unless "the vast majority" of church members support the move. "Be careful," he said, "that we do not run into making rash decisions that can deeply divide the church and weaken its effectiveness."[17] Carey's opposition to the ordination of homosexuals was apparently based not on biblical truth but on a desire to avoid division.

So rampant is the new tolerance in the church today that biblical standards are being ignored—or redrawn—in favor of a more "tolerant" approach . . . one that seeks to redefine marriage and sexuality according to human standards and "sensibilities." In time, this so-called tolerant approach threatens to make you, your church, and your children more accepting of behavior and a lifestyle that God's Word calls "an abomination" (Leviticus 18:22; 20:13, KJV).

But it is possible to respond in Christlike fashion to these changes and challenges, if we are careful to *aggressively* live in love and *humbly* stand for truth. That process may be helped by the following suggestions:

• Prayerfully and patiently consider God's will. Even
within the church, the response of Christians has too often been to separate from those with transparent agen-
das or questionable views. We have sought to preserve
the purity of the church by avoiding seminaries, denominations, churches, groups, and individuals who espouse unbiblical ideas. The salt has fled the saltshaker.

If we are to stand for biblical Christianity, perhaps we
should begin by cultivating strong, healthy relationships
with those on both sides of the issues—even those on the
wrong side! There is an inherent risk in this, I know; salt
can lose its saltiness and become worthless (Matthew
5:13). But salt that never salts anything is also worthless.

A fine evangelical Presbyterian church near my home
has recently undergone a traumatic time of struggle and
transition. Some of the members and staff, concerned by
their denomination's developing positions on homosexuality and the ordination of homosexuals, decided to leave
the church and establish a new congregation; other concerned members and staff resolved to stay behind and
strive to be a witness to biblical Christianity within the denomination (while withholding their funds from de-
nominational agencies and ignoring some church
mandates).

I grieve over a dynamic church split apart by the forces
of the new tolerance in its denomination. I am sympathetic to those who felt the time had come to make a cou-
rageous statement by leaving the denomination and
congregation they had loved for many years. But I am also
heartened by the courage of those who stayed because I
am convinced that relationship is vital to the cause of

Christ in combatting the new tolerance that threatens to destroy his church.

- Remember that those within the church are susceptible to the same needs as those outside the church. Such needs include

  - the need for acceptance, to feel a part of some cause or some group;
  - the need for affection, the desire to be liked and to feel liked;
  - the need for approval, the need to have one's behavior pronounced good;
  - the need for attention, the desire to be noticed;
  - the need for support;
  - the need for respect.

  These needs and others often motivate those within the church to jump aboard the "tolerance" bandwagon. A seminary professor may—consciously or unconsciously—undermine the authority and inspiration of the Bible, knowing that his writings will gain far more acceptance in academia. Or a pastor may take a permissive view toward homosexual unions in an effort—conscious or subconscious—to appear more caring and compassionate.

  Such illegitimate responses to legitimate needs may not be excusable, but if we are able to recognize the needs that prompt the behavior, we will be better equipped to deal with the real issues, and not just the symptoms, that combine to cause the walls of the church to crumble.

- Make the most of every opportunity to demonstrate that real Christian love trumps "tolerance" every time. It is difficult to label a Christian a homophobe if he spends

Saturday afternoons sitting by the bedsides of homosexual patients in AIDS wards. It is difficult to accuse a church of bigotry if its members unite across racial lines to rebuild a church destroyed by an arsonist. It is difficult to brand a Christian as intolerant if she demonstrates acceptance to someone who is different from her.

Let me illustrate what I mean by sharing an incident that occurred at a conference where I was speaking. The conference took place at a retreat center that was large enough to accommodate several groups at a time. When our group, a Christian writers conference, entered the cafeteria for our first meal, we were joined by the other group on the campus: fifty or sixty teenagers from a church that ministered to "alternative" kids, some of whom dressed wildly and even lived on the streets.

In the cafeteria line ahead of me stood a white-haired lady who was attending the writers conference. In front of *her* was a young woman about eighteen or nineteen years old, wildly dressed, and sporting a spiked hairdo of (seemingly) a thousand different colors.

I watched with interest as the older woman examined the girl's appearance, then reached out to tap her on the shoulder. I held my breath.

The older woman spoke in a tremulous but clear voice. "I *love* your hair!" she said, smiling broadly and pointing admiringly at the girl's coiffure. The young woman smiled back, and the two struck up a conversation that lasted through most of the meal.

That Christian woman did more than tolerate her companion; she reached out lovingly to her. I don't know whether she approved of the rest of the girl's appearance. I don't know whether or not she recognized a need for attention in the girl. But she apparently found something she liked, and in so doing discovered a way to give the girl what she craved. This woman's warm (and unexpected) response apparently struck a chord with the girl—and with me.

Children of Lesser Gods

Not long ago, Brett Hershey came home with a friend from his basketball team. A Muslim friend.

Brett and his parents are Christians. They attend an evangelical Christian church. They live in a small Midwestern community. And they are surrounded by kids and families who are involved in non-Christian religions and the "new" spiritualities such as Eastern mysticism, the New Age movement, and others.

This is one of the most profound changes of the past twenty years in Western society. Christine Wicker, writing in *The Dallas Morning News,* says that "what sets American teenagers today apart from teens of previous generations is that their experience with people of other faiths is so much broader."[18]

Not only do you and your children live in a much more pluralistic society, but according to Emory University's Don C. Richter, director of a summer "theology academy" for teens, Christian kids "are very concerned about the exclusivist claims of Christianity, the idea that Jesus is the way and the light and 'no one comes to the Father except by me.'"[19]

Such concerns exist not only among Christian teens today; they are reflected in the rest of the church as well. One of the most portentous effects of the new tolerance on the church today is seen in the rejection of "Christian exclusivism," which is best defined by Professor J. Robert Nelson of Oberlin College:

> Here is where the uniqueness lies. The Lord our God is one Lord; and this one God has entered into the stream of human history in one way, in one man, at one time, for the sake of all men in all times. That is the very nucleus of the Christian affirmation of faith.[20]

Many voices from within the church seem to be calling for the rejection of that affirmation, not primarily because it asserts the truth of Christianity, but because it must necessarily assert the falsity of all contrary doctrines (and that, of course, runs counter to the new tolerance). Missionary Harold Netland explains that "Christian exclusivism does not entail that *none* of the claims made by other religious traditions are true. But what it does deny is that beliefs of other traditions can be true when they are incompatible with those derived from Scripture."[21]

And in a society dominated by the new tolerance, it is just there that problems arise. In his book entitled *Christ's Lordship and Religious Pluralism*, W. Cantwell Smith states:

> Exclusivism strikes more and more Christians as immoral. If the head proves it true, while the heart sees it as wicked, un-Christian, then should Christians not follow the heart? Maybe this is the crux of our dilemma.[22]

According to Paul Knitter, in his book *No Other Name? (A Critical Survey of Christian Attitudes toward Other Religions)*:

> The conservative Evangelical declaration that there can be authentic, reliable revelation only in Christ simply does not hold up in light of the faith, dedication, love, and

peace that Christians find in the teachings and especially in the followers of other religions.[23]

Bill Phipps, moderator of the United Church of Canada, that nation's largest Protestant denomination, said recently "that he did not believe Jesus Christ was God, was bodily resurrected, or was the only way to God." After his remarks caused an outcry within the denomination, the UCC's seventy-member lay and clergy council announced that his comments fell "well within the spectrum of the United Church."[24]

Do you see what is happening? Voices *within the church* are calling upon Christians to abandon their stubborn insistence that Jesus is the only way to salvation, the only name by which we may be saved (John 14:6; Acts 4:12). Voices *within the church* are trying to persuade us and our children that Christianity is no different, nor more true, than any other faith.

As Christ's church strives to come to terms with the world, Søren Kierkegaard's words echo ominously, warning of the result of such unholy compromise with the new tolerance: "Christianity is abolished."[25]

Your children are growing up in a different church than the one in which you grew up. According to Richter, they are far more likely to say, "Why is the Bible any more authoritative than the Bhagavad Gita and the Koran?" They'll say something to the effect that, "I have this Buddhist friend or this Muslim friend, and they're better than I am, and if they aren't going to heaven, I'm not sure I am," he says. The new tolerance that has crept into the church threatens their assurance of salvation, their belief in the Bible, and ultimately their faith in a Christ who is the only way to salvation. The tolerance that exists in the church today may even encourage them to seek salvation somewhere else . . . thus endangering their eternal souls.

How do we counter such dangers? How do we prevent the siren song of new tolerance from seducing our children away from the faith? It begins, I believe, with the realization that the task of rebuilding the crumbling walls of the church, in J. B. Cheaney's words, is not our task alone. It is Christ's church, after all, and he will build his church (Matthew 16:18). But just as the walls of the church have crumbled one brick at a time, so we may play a part in rebuilding them . . . brick by brick, in ways such as the following:

- Keep in mind, as mentioned in chapter 7, that the church is *the most multicultural institution* in the world. Realization of this fact ought to encourage implementation of Peter Tze Ming Ng's suggestion to "encourage the development of curriculum, Bible studies, and worship materials that emphasize the pluralistic nature of the Christian faith."[26]

- Expose your children to basic critical-thinking concepts such as the law of noncontradiction (two contrary positions cannot be true, but both can be false) and the three-step process (understand, evaluate, respond) discussed in chapter 9.

- Recognize the arrogance of a position that says, "It is arrogant to claim that Christianity is unique." The person who assumes that Christian exclusivism is inherently arrogant and morally blameworthy is certainly no less arrogant than those he or she accuses of arrogance. Such an individual is doing exactly what he or she accuses

Christians of doing—pronouncing judgment on the attitudes and actions of someone else!

- Don't try to shelter your children or keep them insu-
  lated from other religions; instead, carefully expose
  them to non-Christian religions in a way that teaches
  them to discern between biblical and nonbiblical ideas,
  between what is harmless and what is dangerous. One
  way to do this is to make your home a safe, comfortable
  place for them to bring their friends home, including
  non-Christian friends, because in that context you can
  help your kids understand and evaluate what the other
  kids think and believe. And make sure you consistently
  communicate that everyone—whatever his or her
  faith—is someone made in God's image, a priceless soul
  for whom Christ died.

  For example, Brett Hershey's father, a campus director
  for Campus Crusade for Christ, not only accepted his
  son's Muslim friend but he sat down with him and began
  asking questions about Islam while Brett watched and listened. After probing his son's friend about his faith, he
  asked for permission to explain what Christians believe.
  His approach not only exposed Brett to Islam in a safe way
  that helped him evaluate his friend's faith but also provided an opportunity for the friend to hear about Christ.

- If your children express interest in one of the non-
  Christian religions or spiritualities, don't try to suppress
  his or her curiosity; instead, seek to understand what is
  attracting him or her. Ask yourself, *What do they find in-
  teresting or fascinating about it? Are they trying to meet a
  need or fill a void of some kind?* Charles Strohmer, author
  of *The Gospel and the New Spirituality,* says, "Too often

parents try to suppress their child's curiosity instead of understanding it." It's better, he says, to "assess the reasons this view or tradition fascinates this person, and look for the truth that answers the lie. It's better to say, 'You're interested in reincarnation? Oh, well, that's probably because you're interested in the afterlife. Let's talk about that.' That way you're talking about what interests the child or the young person, instead of criticizing him or her."[27]

- Strive for the spirit described by Harold Netland, an Evangelical Free Church missionary in Japan:

> Christian exclusivism certainly cannot boast of exhaustive knowledge of God. There is a vast sum of knowledge about God and the world of which we are unaware. And finally, there is no room [in] exclusivism, properly understood, for any pride or arrogant triumphalism. All of us are, at best, no more than sinners saved by God's grace. Nor should we forget that adherents of other religious traditions are, like us, created in God's image and the objects of God's limitless and unfathomable love. Humility and genuine respect should characterize our interaction with those of other faiths.[28]

- Don't suppose you have to oppose *everything* that hints of "tolerance" in the church. For example, while Christians should guard against any suggestion that all cultures, cultural practices, and truth claims are equally valid, non-Western approaches to worship (singing in languages other than English, using non-Western instruments, etc.) and church missions can be very helpful and appropriate. And American believers need to humbly acknowledge that while we have much to share with other cultures, we have much to learn from them as well.

• Remember that Jesus answered his critics by dying for them as well as for his followers. His followers can do no better than to selflessly love and bless those who oppose the church and the gospel (Proverbs 25:21-22; Romans 12:20).

Chapter 11

SHINING LIKE STARS

When Joan first met Robert, she was less than enthusiastic about working with him. And Robert's opening words to her made the situation appear even less promising.

"I just want you to know that I hate people like you," he said.

Joan, a professional writer, had been engrossed in a fascinating and rewarding project when she sensed God calling her to put her work aside for something else. She had no idea what it was God wanted her to do, but after a few feeble arguments and rationalizations, she gave in.

Not long afterward, she awoke one morning with the crystal-clear impression that she should write a novel depicting God's love and grace toward a Christian family torn apart by the revelation that one of its members was homosexual and had contracted AIDS, at that time a relatively new but deadly disease.

Why should I do that? she wondered. *I don't know anyone with the disease, nor, to be perfectly honest, do I have any desire to.*

That night she saw in the newspaper a letter to the editor

from a young man named Robert. Robert was angry. He was dying. And he had AIDS.

Joan found Robert's number and called him. Feeling a bit foolish, she explained to him that she was a Christian and that she believed God had called her to write a book about AIDS. Would he help her?

After a moment of silence, Robert responded. "Sure," he said. "I'll help you. But only because I want to make sure you get it right. And I have one condition: no preaching!"

Joan agreed, and they met for lunch. No sooner had they taken their seats at a table by the window, however, than Robert opened the conversation with his angry comment.

Stunned, Joan could only ask why.

"I hate people like you," Robert explained, "because it's your fault I have AIDS—all you self-righteous religious fanatics and your so-called rules. If it weren't for you, we gays could get married just like anybody else, and we never would have gotten involved in all these multiple relationships and put ourselves at risk for things like AIDS."

Before Joan could respond, he went on, listing his grievances against the world—specifically, Christians. His language was peppered with profanity and steeped in sarcasm and bitterness.

As she sat silently absorbing his hateful discourse, Joan found herself questioning God. Why would he allow her to be subjected to such verbal abuse? What possible good could come from such a relationship? What purpose could there be for her writing a book about AIDS? Couldn't someone else do the job? At the very least, there had to be someone more agreeable than Robert to help with the project. Joan resolved to finish the meeting as quickly as possible and tell Robert she had decided not to work with him after all.

And then Robert stopped—just for a moment—and glanced out the window. When he looked back there was a hint of tears in his pale blue eyes. "Sometimes," he said, his voice barely above a whisper, "I wonder if people like you are right." And then he returned to his angry demeanor.

For a split second, God had allowed Joan to catch a glimpse of a chink in Robert's armor. It was all she needed. Honoring her promise not to "preach" at him, they dove into the project and worked together on the manuscript for many months. Joan would draft a chapter, weaving the message of God's love and grace into the fabric of the story. Then Robert would read it and give her his thoughts and comments. But the vulnerability she glimpsed in the coffee shop was never repeated. Robert continued to express only hostility toward God and Christians, though he was seldom unkind to Joan.

By the time Joan was writing the final chapter, Robert was on his deathbed, barely able to lift the pages she sent him to read. Then one day he called her.

"Joan," he said, struggling to breathe, "do you really believe all that Jesus stuff, all that stuff about love and forgiveness, heaven and hell?"

"Yes," she whispered into the phone. "I really do, Robert."

"Then you've got five minutes to tell me why I shouldn't kill myself and end it all right now."

It took more than five minutes, but before Joan hung up her phone later that afternoon, she had led Robert in the sinner's prayer. The young man who hated Christians had become one. Two weeks later he died. His last words were, "I can't wait to go home and see Jesus." When the organist played "Amazing Grace" at his funeral, Joan sat next to Robert's mother and wept—not just because she missed her friend, but because she had learned more about love and grace in the few months she had known Robert than in all the years she had heard it preached in church.

IMPARTING OUR VERY LIVES

Joan's story is true. It is also an illustration of how real Christlike love works—even in the age of the new tolerance. I believe it was this kind of love in action, Paul the apostle described when he told the Thessalonian Christians, "We proved to be gentle among you, as a nursing mother tenderly cares for her own children. Having thus a fond affection for you, we were well-pleased *to impart to you not only the gospel of God but also our own lives*" (1 Thessalonians 2:7-8, NASB, italics added).

Paul and his team imparted not only the gospel but *their very lives.* What does that mean? It is similar to what Christ did, as John describes it: "The Word became flesh and made his dwelling among us" (John 1:14). Jesus did not only send the gospel; he did not just preach the good news. He became flesh. He came down to our level. He experienced humanity. He lived among us. He hurt with us. He cried with us. He laughed with us. He gave his life for us and imparted his life to us.

Since that same Christ dwells in us, we are empowered to do more than preach the gospel with logical presentations and persuasive arguments. When the Word of truth is made part of our very lives we can impart that truth relationally as well as with our words.

David Ferguson of Intimate Life Ministries is a pioneer in this area of teaching Christian leaders how to impart our lives to those around us. In his *Great Commandment Ministry Workbook* he says,

When the living Word is experienced in our lives and acted upon in our relationships with others, we are in fact imparting our lives to others. Truth can often be studied and eloquently proclaimed with minimal impact. But when truth is internalized and made a living epistle and then imparted through the teacher's life, it carries with it the authority and power of God. It is no longer just ideas and thoughts from an authoritative book, it is actually the truth of God ministered through the life of a "humble servant through the power of God's Spirit."

When you lovingly and humbly comfort your child, your spouse or a friend in the power of 2 Cor. 1:3-4, you are imparting your life to that person. When you lovingly and humbly give attention to a friend or stranger or a loved one in the power of 1 Cor. 12:25, you are imparting your life to that person. When you lovingly and humbly give support to one in need in the power of Gal. 6:2, you are imparting your life to that person.[1]

Friendships and relationships are not merely means to an end—the end being a gospel presentation. When the Word became flesh, truth actually became relational in the person of Jesus Christ. We must, in many respects, redefine what it means to share Christ. We must do more than embrace or preach truth as a concept. To reach others—even our own children—in this age of the new tolerance we must impart the gospel by sharing our very lives . . . just as Jesus did.

A NEW APOLOGETIC

I have spent much of my life documenting the evidences of our faith. I have tried to follow Peter's admonition of "always being ready to make a defense to everyone who asks you to give an account for the hope that is in you" (1 Peter 3:15, NASB). But because of the widespread influence of the new tolerance, I have discovered that the truth of the faith—and the evidences that testify to its truth—is increasingly becoming a nonissue these days. Fewer and fewer people are asking questions that can be answered with evidential apologetics. Yet those questions need to be asked—and answered. But in our postmodern, relativistic culture, an emphasis on "what is true" has decreased and an interest in "what works" has increased.

I'm convinced that the vast majority of young people who are becoming Christians today are coming to the faith not so much because it is true and credible but because it is the best thing presented to them to date. And, as a result, I can virtually guarantee you that when something else comes along that appears better, they'll be drawn away and will abandon the faith.

Because of the new tolerance, our culture today is not so much asking whether the gospel is credible; it is asking whether the gospel is relevant. And if we are to attract a needy world to Christ, we must demonstrate that he is both *evidentially credible* and *relationally relevant.* That means we must adopt a new apologetic, a new defense, that shows the faith to be both *credible* and *relevant.* And I believe that if we are to do that, we must concentrate new efforts in at least five areas:

1. Develop Community

A new commandment I give to you, that you love one another, even as I have loved you, that you also love one another. By this all men will know that you are My disciples, if you have love for one another." (John 13:34-35, NASB)

I don't have to tell you we live in a love-starved world. A composite of several studies reveals that 80 to 85 percent of our adult population grew up suffering from some form of parental separation or physical or sexual abuse or have been exposed to some type of parental addictive behavior.[2] And while a hurting generation needs to hear the gospel message of salvation in Christ, they also need to hear and see the truth of the gospel being lived in and through a community of people who are truly loving one another and demonstrating a biblical model of relationships.

True Christian community—what the New Testament calls *koinonia*—is powerfully attractive and winsome. As our children and the world hear and see us lovingly sharing our lives with one another—eating in one another's homes, sharing material blessings with each other, supporting and encouraging each other, praying together, weeping together, celebrating together—they will want to know, "Where do you get such love?" When we are relationally relevant, we not only have the opportunity to point them to the source of that love but we can also share the evidence that demonstrates that he is the one and only true source of love.

2. Show Compassion

Happy are those who have the God of Israel as their helper, whose hope is in the Lord their God. He is the one who made heaven and earth, the sea, and everything in them. He is the one who keeps every promise forever, who gives justice to the oppressed and food to the hungry. . . . The Lord protects the foreigners among us. He cares for the orphans and widows. (Psalm 146:5-9, NLT)

We serve "the Father of compassion and the God of all comfort" (2 Corinthians 1:3), a God who is "full of compassion" (Psalm 116:5). And when we reach out to the widows, the fatherless, the homeless, the poor, and the needy, we reflect the nature of God and become ministers of his manifold grace (1 Peter 4:10).

Unfortunately, however, I'm afraid we in the church have too often relinquished our responsibility to care for those in need or attempted to delegate our responsibility to government programs and social agencies. We must recapture the heart of a compassionate God "who comforts us in all our affliction so that we may be able to comfort those who are in any affliction" (2 Corinthians 1:4, NASB).

Even a culture dominated by the new tolerance will find it difficult to resist the compassionate heart of a believer and follower of the one true God. We will more often gain a hearing as we impart the truth of God by compassionately caring for the needs of others.

3. Protect Creation

God said to them, "Be fruitful and multiply, and fill the earth, and subdue it; and rule over the fish of the sea and over the birds of the sky, and over every living thing that moves on the earth." (Genesis 1:28, NASB)

Then the Lord God took the man and put him into the garden of Eden to cultivate it and keep it. (Genesis 2:15, NASB)

It may seem strange to suggest that a concern for creation—that is, the environment—could have anything to do with demonstrating an evidentially credible and relationally relevant faith. But I am convinced that this is yet another area in which we, the people of God, have neglected or abrogated our responsibility.

When God said to subdue the earth, he didn't mean to pollute and destroy it; the wonders and beauties of his creation are a priceless trust, and that biblical truth presents us with an effectual door of ministry (2 Corinthians 2:12) to those in the culture around us who are concerned with how humans are using and misusing our planet. When we show respect and concern for God's creation we gain a hearing with today's environmentally conscious generation.

4. Model Close Marital and Family Relationships

Husbands, love your wives, just as Christ also loved the church and gave Himself up for her. . . . So husbands ought also to love their own wives as their own bodies. He who loves his own wife loves himself; for no one ever hated his own flesh, but nourishes and cherishes it, just as Christ also does the church, because we are members of His body. For this cause a man shall leave his father and mother, and shall cleave to his wife; and the two shall become one flesh. (Ephesians 5:25-31, NASB)

The divinely ordained relationship of marriage and the family is God's beautiful showcase of unity and oneness. In fact, Christ's love that led him to sacrifice himself for the church is the model and word picture for marriage. It is no wonder, then, that God wants to use marriage and the family to attract people to himself.

Study after study shows that young people today overwhelmingly want a happy home life. Our own 1994 study of churched youth revealed that out of a list of fifteen desirable conditions, 85 percent chose "one marriage partner for life" as their number one desire.[3] They picked that over "good physical health," "a close relationship with God," "having a comfortable lifestyle," etc.

If we hope to effectively influence others—even our own children—in today's culture, I believe the church must show that the Christian faith is not only credible but also relevant to healthy and rewarding marriages and families. As the relational relevance of the gospel is lived out within our marriages and families, we will be giving "a defense . . . for the hope that is in [us]" (1 Peter 3:15, NASB) to a generation that might otherwise be unconvinced of its need for Christ.

5. Offer a Compelling Personal Testimony

Now the salvation, and the power, and the kingdom of our God and the authority of His Christ have come, for the accuser of our brethren has been thrown down, who accuses them before our God day and night. And they overcame him because of the blood of the Lamb and because of the word of their testimony. (Revelation 12:10-11, NASB)

The new tolerance places a premium on personal experience. The question "Is it true?" has been replaced by "Will it work for me?"

Christians can respond to this postmodern situation by taking every opportunity to share our personal testimonies and tell others how the gospel of God's transforming grace has changed our lives. After thirty years of public ministry, I have discovered during the past several years that my personal testimony of Christ's love and forgiveness is more effective than ever.

Imparting our lives to a needy world in these times will involve personal testimony as much as, if not more than, ever before in the history of the church.

SHARING THE GOSPEL IN LOVE THROUGH OUR LIVES

Sharing the gospel and imparting our very lives to those around us is not an either/or proposition; we need not choose between one or the other.

Neither is this task of imparting our lives a matter of *before and after*. It is not something we do in order to get to the "real" task of personal evangelism.

When I speak of imparting our very lives, I am talking about taking the initiative to share the truth of God's love and forgiveness *in the context of relationships.*

Our commission is to "go and make disciples" (Matthew 28:19). The command is to "make disciples." But we are to make those disciples "as we go." We are to impart the gospel and our lives to all those with whom we make contact.

The relevant church—we who are of Christ's body—have the great privilege to launch the twenty-first century by both sharing Christ's message and imparting our very lives. The more relationally relevant Christ's message is to our own lives, the more attractive the gospel will be to a needy world. And the more attractive and relevant that message is, the greater chance we will have to demonstrate how the one true God is evidentially credible.

I believe God is calling his church in this age of the new tolerance to aggressively live in love and humbly stand for truth. I believe he is calling us to demonstrate what real love looks like by becoming a people who share a message that is evidentially credible and relationally relevant. And I believe he is calling each of us to launch the twenty-first century with a Holy Spirit–led, Holy Spirit–empowered harvest of souls.

Hosanna Industries is an example of what I mean. This Presbyterian housing ministry recently assembled one hundred volunteers from twelve states to rebuild—in one week—Saint Mark's Missionary Baptist Church, the home of a predominantly African-American congregation that had been destroyed by arson.[4]

The churches of Oxford, Ohio, are another example of a vibrant, imaginative response to God's call. A local auto dealership banded together with several congregations one Saturday in an interchurch and interracial effort, providing free oil changes and spark-plug replacement to widows and single mothers. The participating groups even refused donations that were offered, explaining that they were motivated by Christian love and a desire to serve.

A determined woman attending an evangelism conference in Houston, Texas, demonstrated what God intends for his church. When she and others in her "street witnessing" group went to a local park frequented by joggers, the joggers ignored them and the police asked them to disperse. Just as they were preparing to leave, however, the woman announced that she had an idea, hopped into her car, and drove off. She quickly returned—with twenty dozen Popsicles! "I just thought that there was probably no law against giving out Popsicles without a permit." Within twenty minutes, the Popsicles were gone, but a number of joggers had stopped to talk while they ate their free Popsicle, and some even asked, "What kind of Christians are you, anyway?"[5]

Questions like that will be generated by real Christian love—love that not only imparts the gospel but also imparts our very lives to those around us. It is a love that accepts the person regardless of his or her beliefs or behavior; a love that seeks to meet needs and to protect and provide for each person's health, happiness, and spiritual growth; a love that will speak the truth but will not minister condemnation or neglect a person's needs.

It's that kind of love that motivates Christian volunteers with Voice of Calvary Ministries to renovate sixty-five houses in one neighborhood in Jackson, Mississippi (and thirty-five houses in another neighborhood!), providing affordable housing, home-ownership training, and spiritual counseling to low-income families.[6]

It's that kind of love that prompted Kim Davison to become involved with Love & Action, a ministry to AIDS patients in Annapolis, Maryland. Kim, who was HIV-positive herself, "initiated an annual drive to gather like-new stuffed animals for HIV-positive adults and children." Upon her death, the stuffed-animal effort was renamed "Kim's Teddy Bear Campaign."[7]

It's that kind of love that prompted ninety-year-old Pauline Hord to teach hundreds of prison inmates to read[8] and motivated Jim and Terri Cooney to adopt seven "rainbow" children—"African, Mexican, Caucasian, unknown"—many of whom have mood and behavior disorders.[9]

If you and I, Christian men and women, aggressively live in love while humbly standing for truth, the imparting of the gospel and our lives will not only silence the militant critics of the faith and opponents of biblical morality; we will, by God's power and grace, see even greater things come to pass. Just as Robert the Christian-hater became Robert the Christian and just as Saul the persecutor of the church became Paul the planter of churches, so, God willing, some of our most bitter enemies will someday become friends of God—and our brothers and sisters in Christ.

After all, the only way to truly eliminate an enemy is to make him a friend. That is what God did with us; when we were God's enemies, the Bible says, he "reconciled us to himself through Christ and gave us the ministry of reconciliation: that God was reconciling the world to himself in Christ, not counting men's sins against them. And he has committed to us the message of reconciliation. We are therefore Christ's ambassadors, as though God were making his appeal through us" (2 Corinthians 5:18-20).

As Chuck Colson has said, "This is our greatest apologetic—living the truth out in love."[10] May God help us to answer his call and rise to the challenge.

> *Those who are wise will shine like the brightness of the heavens, and those who lead many to righteousness, like the stars for ever and ever. (Daniel 12:3)*

GLOSSARY OF TERMS

ETHICAL THEISM
A worldview characterized by the belief that right and wrong are absolute, unchanging, and decided (and communicated to men and women) by God.

EXCLUSIVISM
Applied primarily to Christians; the belief that Jesus is the only way to salvation; that the Bible is God's true, authoritative, and definitive self-revelation; and that where the claims of Scripture are incompatible with those of other faiths, the latter are not to be accepted as truth.[1]

INCLUSIVISM
The view that "there is only one true religion through which salvation may be obtained. . . . But God may impute salvation to the sincere worshipper of false gods. Although those in other religions may refuse to partake from (or not know about) the proper religious diet, God will not let them starve."[2]

MODERNISM
A worldview that emphasizes "rationality (the ability of humans to understand their world), empiricism (the belief that knowledge can only be gained through our senses), and . . . the application of rationality and empiricism through science and technology."[3] To a modernist, any

truth that cannot be observed and experienced—such as spiritual or moral truth—is *relative* (that is, different from person to person).

MULTICULTURALISM
The promotion of familiarity with and acceptance of different cultures, based on the assumption that truth is culturally based. "Multiculturalists argue that since there are multiple descriptions of reality, no one view can be true in an ultimate sense. . . . [They believe that] no truth transcends culture, that no idea or moral concept might be true for every cultural group, or every human being."[4]

NEW TOLERANCE
"The definition of *new . . . tolerance* is that every individual's beliefs, values, lifestyle, and perception of truth claims are equal. . . . There is no hierarchy of truth. Your beliefs and my beliefs are equal and all truth is relative."[5]

POLITICAL CORRECTNESS
Behavior or belief that is approved or accepted when measured by the standards of the new tolerance (postmodernism, multiculturalism, and universalism).

PLURALISM
A condition that exists when a society possesses many different religions, worldviews, and truth claims and none is dominant. Also used as a synonym for *universalism* (below).

POSTMODERNISM
A worldview characterized by the belief that truth doesn't exist in any objective sense but is created rather than discovered. Postmodernists "think things like reason, rationality, and confidence in science are cultural biases."[6] Truth—whether in science, education, or religion—is created by the specific culture and exists only in that culture. Therefore, any system or statement that tries to communicate truth is a power play, an effort to dominate other cultures.

UNIVERSALISM
A view of religion that "says (positively) all worldviews can be valid avenues of salvation and (negatively) exclusivism is wrong."[7]

ENDNOTES

CHAPTER 1—A GROWING THREAT

1. *Webster's New World Dictionary of English,* 3rd ed., s.v "tolerate."
2. Monica and Sherry's story is fictional, but it is based on several true experiences that have been related to the authors.
3. News release, The Rutherford Institute, 26 March 1997.
4. Brigid McMenamin, "The PC Enforcers," *Forbes* (10 February 1997): 86.
5. Jay Sekulow and Keith Fournier, *And Nothing but the Truth* (Atlanta: Thomas Nelson, 1996), 82.
6. Brannon Howse, "The People and Agenda of Multicultural Education," *Understanding the Times* (January 1997): 3.
7. Chuck Colson, "Facilitating Faith (Do We Need a Prayer Amendment?)," *BreakPoint,* 8 February 1995.
8. Personal experience related to Steve Brown, researcher for Josh McDowell Ministry.
9. "Christianity under Attack," The Rutherford Institute, http://www.rutherford.org/central.html.
10. "Christianity under Attack," The Rutherford Institute, http://www.rutherford.org/ne. html.
11. "Christianity under Attack," The Rutherford Institute, http://www.rutherford.org/ne. html, p. 4.

12. Dennis McCallum, "Are We Ready?," *The Death of Truth*, ed. Dennis McCallum (Minneapolis: Bethany House, 1996), 12.

CHAPTER 2—TWO KINDS OF TOLERANCE

1. *Webster's New World Dictionary of English*, 3rd ed., s.v. "tolerate."
2. John 4:1-42
3. Luke 19:1-10
4. Matthew 8:1-4
5. Matthew 15:21-28
6. Stanley J. Grenz, *A Primer to Postmodernism* (Grand Rapids: Wm. B. Eerdmans, 1996), 14.
7. Don Closson, "Multiculturalism," *Probe Perspectives* (Richardson, Tex.: Probe Ministries, n.d.): 1.
8. Fernando Savater, *El Mito Nacionalista* (Madrid: Alianza Editorial, 1996), 16–19.
9. Thomas A. Helmbock, "Insights on Tolerance," *Cross and Crescent* (the publication of Lambda Chi Alpha International Fraternity), summer 1996, 2.
10. Edwin J. Delattre, "Diversity, Ethics, and Education in America," *Ethics: Easier Said than Done,* Joseph & Edna Josephson Institute, 48–51.
11. Stephen Bates, "Religious Diversity and the Schools," *The American Enterprise* 4, no. 5 (September/October 1993): 18.
12. Edwin J. Delattre, "Diversity, Ethics, and Education in America," 49.
13. Personal correspondence with Josh McDowell.
14. Josh McDowell and Bob Hostetler, *Right From Wrong* (Dallas: Word Publishing, 1994), 15.
15. "Flexible Ethics: It Depends," USA Snapshots, *USA Today*, 29 April 1997.
16. Dr. James Banks, *An Introduction to Multicultural Education* (Boston: Allyn & Bacon, 1994).
17. Edwin J. Delattre, "Diversity, Ethics, and Education in America," 48–51.
18. E. Calvin Beisner, "The Double-Edged Sword of Multiculturalism," *The Freeman* (March 1994): 109.

19. Ibid., 109–10.
20. John Leo, *Washington Times*, as quoted in "That's Outrageous! (It's All Relative)," *Reader's Digest* 152, no. 910 (February 1998): 75.
21. John Leo, "Heather Has a Message," *U.S. News & World Report* 113, no. 7 (17 August 1992): 16.
22. David O. Sacks and Peter A. Thiel, *The Diversity Myth* (Oakland: The Independent Institute, 1995), 176.
23. Richard Bernstein, *Dictatorship of Virtue: Multiculturalism and the Battle for America's Future* (New York: Alfred A. Knopf, 1994), 75.
24. "Christianity under Attack," The Rutherford Institute, http://www.rutherford.org/central. html, 3.
25. "Christianity under Attack," The Rutherford Institute, http://www.rutherford.org/west. html, 3.
26. "Christianity under Attack," The Rutherford Institute, http://www.rutherford.org/southw. html, 1.

CHAPTER 3—THE COST OF TOLERANCE

1. Richard Bernstein, *Dictatorship of Virtue: Multiculturalism and the Battle for America's Future* (New York: Alfred A. Knopf, 1994), 90.
2. "Christianity under Attack," The Rutherford Institute, http://www.rutherford.org/ne. html, 4.
3. "Christianity under Attack," The Rutherford Institute, http://www.rutherford.org/central. html, 1.
4. David F. Wells, *No Place for Truth* (Grand Rapids: Wm. B. Eerdmans, 1993), 259–60.
5. Adapted from *Right From Wrong* by Josh McDowell and Bob Hostetler (Dallas: Word, 1994), 29–31.
6. Dennis McCallum, "Are We Ready?" *The Death of Truth*, ed. Dennis McCallum (Minneapolis: Bethany House, 1996), 13.
7. Stanley J. Grenz, *A Primer to Postmodernism* (Grand Rapids: Wm. B. Eerdmans, 1996), 17.
8. Jean-Francois Lyotard, *The Postmodern Condition: A Report on Knowledge*, trans. Geoff Bennington and Brian Massumi (Minneapolis: University of Minnesota Press, 1984), xxiv.
9. Jim Leffel, "Our New Challenge: Postmodernism," *The Death of*

Truth, ed. Dennis McCallum (Minneapolis: Bethany House, 1996), 35.

10. Ibid., 40.
11. Gene Edward Veith, *Postmodern Times* (Wheaton, Ill.: Crossway, 1994), 13.
12. Jim Leffel, "Our Old Challenge: Modernism," *The Death of Truth,* ed. Dennis McCallum (Minneapolis: Bethany House, 1996), 21.
13. Andres Serrano's "Piss Christ," an "artwork" sponsored by the National Endowment for the Arts (NEA).
14. Tony Snow, "Christmas in Public Is No Crime," *The Cincinnati Enquirer,* 23 December 1997.
15. Inside D.C., Gary L. Bauer, Family Research Council, "Bashers, Bombers and Bigots," *Washington Watch,* 26 March 1996, 4.
16. Edgard Pisani, "Against Intolerance," *The Unesco Courier,* June 1992, 38.
17. Bruce B. Suttle, "The Need for and Inevitability of Educational Intolerance," manuscript.
18. Kim Sue Lia Perkes, "Baptist Group May Shun Austin Church," *The Austin American Statesman,* 10 February 1998.
19. Ryszard Legutko, "The Trouble with Toleration," *Partisan Review* 61, no. 4 (1994): 617.
20. Stephen Bates, "Religious Diversity and the Schools," *The American Enterprise* 4, no. 5 (September/October 1993): 19.
21. Bob Harvey, "Wanted: Old Fashioned Virtue," *Montreal Gazette,* 19 February 1995.
22. "Declaration of Principles on Tolerance," The Member States of the United Nations Educational, Scientific and Cultural Organization, meeting in Paris at the twenty-eighth session of the General Conference, from 25 October to 16 November 1995.
23. Ryszard Legutko, "The Trouble with Toleration," 619.
24. Ibid., 620.
25. Jay Sekulow and Keith Fournier, *And Nothing but the Truth* (Atlanta: Thomas Nelson, 1996), 44. Upon learning of the principal's ruling, the girl's family pressed the issue and finally secured Audrey's right to read her Bible on the school bus.

26. Brannon Howse, "The People and Agenda of Multicultural Education," *Understanding the Times* (January 1997): 3.

27. "California Cross Lamp Must Be Kept under a Bushel," *World,* 20 September 1997, 19. San Francisco city supervisors later crafted a plan to sell a third of an acre around the cross to a private group for $26,000, thus allowing the cross to remain. Restrictions were still placed on the lighting of the cross, however, by the plaintiffs, the American Civil Liberties Union and the American Jewish Congress, which brought the suit.

28. "BC Teachers Withhold Accreditation for TWU," *Faith Today,* September/October 1996, 51.

29. Scott Scruggs, "Truth or Tolerance," *Probe Perspectives* (Richardson, Tex.: Probe Ministries, n.d.): 1.

30. James E. Wood Jr., "Tolerance and Truth in Religion," *Journal of Church and State* 24, no. 1 (winter 1992).

31. J. Robert Nelson, "Tolerance, Bigotry, and the Christian Faith," *Religion in Life* 33, no. 4 (autumn 1964).

32. Contradictory religions cannot all be true (for example, if Christianity's claim that "there is no other name under heaven given to men by which we must be saved" (Acts 4:12) is true, the claims of other religions to the contrary cannot also be true).

33. Ravi Zacharias, *Deliver Us from Evil: Restoring the Soul in a Disintegrating Culture* (Dallas: Word, 1996), 66.

CHAPTER 4—THE IMPLICATIONS OF TOLERANCE

1. Brannon Howse, "The People and Agenda of Multicultural Education," *Understanding the Times* (January 1997): 3.

2. John D. Woodbridge, "Culture War Casualties," *Christianity Today* (6 March 1995): 25.

3. Francis Schaeffer, *How Should We Then Live?* (Old Tappan, N.J.: Fleming H. Revell, 1976), 145.

4. Fernando Savater, *El Mito Nacionalista* (Madrid: Alianza Editorial, 1996), 16–19.

5. The widespread rioting and looting were reportedly occasioned by the rage the community felt following an all-White jury's "not

guilty" verdict in the trial of the White police officers accused of brutally assaulting Black motorist Rodney King.

6. Don Closson, "Multiculturalism," *Probe Perspectives* (Richardson, Tex.: Probe Ministries, n.d.): 5.

7. *Merriam-Webster's Collegiate Dictionary*, 10th ed., s.v. "conviction."

8. Jay Sekulow and Keith Fournier, *And Nothing but the Truth* (Atlanta: Thomas Nelson, 1996), 45–46.

9. Ravi Zacharias, in his book, *Deliver Us from Evil: Restoring the Soul in a Disintegrating Culture* (Dallas: Word, 1996), relates an apt illustration of this point:

> A definitive example of this public expulsion of religious ideas can be seen from two historic incidents in the city of Toronto, Canada. In the 1880s the mayor of that city was William Howland. Howland's platform, as he campaigned for office, was one of concern for the city's moral degeneration. He pledged to work toward making it a decent city and ridding it of some of the public vices and trades that victimized its people. His bid was successful, and he left as his legacy the still-used qualifier to the city of Toronto, "Toronto the Good." Ironically, nearly a century later a major moral issue again caused political debate between candidates running for the mayor's post in Toronto. The incumbent was inundated with pleas to reconsider his position on the issue. He staunchly resisted that pressure, stating that most of those who were troubled by his stand were religiously minded people who, he said, "were prejudiced on such matters," and therefore, he would disregard their counsel (p. 57).

10. Chuck Colson, "Underhanded Compliment: Christianity on Campus," *BreakPoint*, 8 March 1993.

11. Chuck Colson, "Not to Remain Silent," *BreakPoint*, 15 June 1995.

12. William A. Henry III, "The Politics of Separation," *Time* (fall 1993): 75.

13. Calvin J. Camp, "Chinese Seek Stability," letter in *USA Today*, 5 November 1997.

14. Andrea Park, as quoted in *The Diversity Myth*, by David O. Sacks and Peter A. Thiel (Oakland: The Independent Institute, 1995), 32.

15. Ryszard Legutko, "The Trouble with Toleration," *Partisan Review* 61, no. 4 (1994): 616.
16. Quoted in "The Politics of Separation," by William A. Henry III, 75.
17. Simopekka Virkkula, "One Man's War," *Books from Finland*, 24 (1990), 45–50.
18. Cited by Charles Colson in *The Body* (Dallas: Word, 1992), 176.
19. Gene Edward Veith, *Postmodern Times* (Wheaton, Ill.: Crossway, 1994), 75.
20. "Ottawa Woman Strolls Topless," *Toronto Star*, 11 May 1997.
21. *Washington Times*, 1 September 1997.
22. Transcript, *Alan Keyes Show Live*, 1 September 1997.
23. "Tragedy, Stranger than Fiction," *Alliance Defense Fund Update*, 17 March 1997.

CHAPTER 5—THE TACTICS OF TOLERANCE

1. 2 Corinthians 4:4
2. John 8:44
3. Romans 1:16
4. Debra J. Saunders, "Diversity Training," *The San Francisco Chronicle*, 23 June 1996.
5. "Who Is Intolerant?" *Campus Alert* 4, no. 2 (January 1996): 1.
6. Debra J. Saunders, "Diversity Training."
7. "CUSA Plays God," editorial in *The Charlatan*, Carleton University, Ottawa, Canada, 16 January 1997.
8. Chuck Colson, "The Six-Second Crime," *BreakPoint*, 9 February 1994.
9. Brannon Howse, *"The People and Agenda,"* 1.
10. Midge Decter, writing in *Commentary*. Quoted by Daniel Levitas in "A. D. L. and the Christian Right," *The Nation*, 19 June 1995, 882.
11. Dinesh D'Souza, "The Visigoths in Tweed," *Forbes* 147, no. 7 (1 April 1997): 84.
12. Mona Charen, "Kwanzaa Not All It's Cracked Up to Be," *Hamilton Journal*, 31 December 1997.
13. Michael Blowen, "Asian Actor Wins Role in 'Miss Saigon,'" *The Boston Globe*, 18 December 1991.

14. Charles Krauthammer, "Quebec and the Death of Diversity," *Time*, (13 November 1995).

15. See chapter 4 of Dennis McCallum's *The Death of Truth* for a cogent explanation of the significance of power in postmodern thought and action.

16. Dawn Gibeau, "RICO Ruling Adds More Fire to Abortion Debate," *National Catholic Reporter*, 4 February 1994, 4.

17. "Evolution's Unbelievers Unwelcome in Science," Focus on the Family *Citizen* (21 January 1991): 14.

18. Ibid., 15.

CHAPTER 6—THE MORE EXCELLENT WAY

1. S. D. Gaede, *When Tolerance Is No Virtue* (Downers Grove, Ill.: InterVarsity, 1993), 47.

2. Matthew 22:29

3. John 8:11

4. Hebrews 4:15

5. Romans 5:8

6. Ephesians 5:2

7. Max Lucado, *In the Grip of Grace* (Dallas: Word, 1996), 30–31.

8. Ibid., 21.

9. John 4:16-26

10. John 8:3-11

11. John Stott, *Romans: God's Good News for the World* (Downers Grove, Ill.: InterVarsity, 1994), 82.

12. "Wretched Right-Wing Refuse," *Furman University Daily*, 27 September 1996, 9.

13. Geevarghese Mar Osthathios, "Conviction of Truth and Tolerance of Love," *International Review of Mission* 74, no. 246 (October 1985): 496.

14. David Ferguson, *The Great Commandment Principle* (Wheaton, Ill.: Tyndale House, 1998).

15. John D. Woodbridge, "Culture War Casualties," *Christianity Today* (6 March 1995): 25–6.

CHAPTER 7—TOLERANCE AND EDUCATION

1. Derived from *Vote of Intolerance*, by Josh McDowell and Ed Stewart (Wheaton, Ill.: Tyndale House, 1997), 234–45.

2. Sara Bullard, *Teaching Tolerance* Magazine (1998). At www.splcenter.org/teachingtolerance/tt-1.html.

3. Ibid.

4. "Curriculum Guidelines for Multicultural Education," *Social Education* 56, no. 5 (September 1992), 277.

5. Kenneth S. Stern, "Battling Bigotry on Campus," *USA Today* 120, no. 2562 (March 1992): 62.

6. Stephen Bates, "Religious Diversity and the Schools," *The American Enterprise* 4, no. 5 (September/October 1993): 18.

7. Personal conversation with Josh McDowell, 7 April 1998.

8. Richard Bernstein, *Dictatorship of Virtue: Multiculturalism and the Battle for America's Future* (New York: Alfred A. Knopf, 1994), 252.

9. Lynn V. Cheney, "Taking Steps to Build Support for Change," *Change* 25, no. 1 (January/February 1993): 8–11.

10. Ibid., 244, 181.

11. Richard Bernstein, *Dictatorship of Virtue*, 283.

12. Quoted by John Zmirak in "Uncommon Ground," *Working at Home* (winter 1998): 90.

13. Ellen Somekawa and Elizabeth A. Smith, "Theorizing the Writing of History or, I Can't Think Why It Should Be So Dull, for a Great Deal of It Must Be Invention," *Journal of Social History* (Fall 1988): 154.

14. Gene Edward Veith, *Postmodern Times*, (Wheaton, Ill.: Crossway, 1994), 50.

15. Adapted from John Leo, "History Standards Are Bunk," *U.S. News & World Report* 118, no. 5 (6 February 1995): 23.

16. Dinesh D'Souza, "The Visigoths in Tweed," *Forbes* 147, no. 7 (1 April 1997): 81.

17. Ibid., 86.

18. Richard Bernstein, *Dictatorship of Virtue*, 263.

19. Ibid., 283.

20. John Leo, "History Standards Are Bunk," *U.S. News & World Report* 118, no. 5 (6 February 1995): 23.

21. S. D. Gaede, *When Tolerance Is No Virtue* (Downers Grove, Ill.: InterVarsity, 1993), 63.

22. Peter Tze Ming Ng, "Toward a New Agenda for Religious Education in a Multicultural Society," *Religious Education* 88, no. 4 (fall 1993): 591.

23. Ibid., 587.

24. Ibid., 63–4.

25. Dinesh D'Souza, "The Visigoths in Tweed," 83.

26. Ibid., 83.

27. Florence King, "The Goading of America," *Chronicles*, May 1991, 26. John Leo of *U.S. News & World Report* called seven prominent Egyptologists at random to ask their opinion on the Black Egypt theory propagated by Afrocentric scholars such as Martin Bernal of Cornell, Asa G. Hilliard of Georgia State, and Theophile J. Obenga of Gabon. All seven said that the theory was "not true," then asked that their names not be used; one explained that it was politically too hot to discuss on the record.

28. Don Feder, "'Multiculturalism' Often Is Much like Reason," *Human Events*, 28 September 1991, 787.

29. Richard Bernstein, *Dictatorship of Virtue*, 277.

30. Chuck Colson, "Facilitating Faith," *BreakPoint*, 8 February 1995.

31. Richard Bernstein, *Dictatorship of Virtue*, 65.

32. Paul Weyrich, "Politically Correct Fascism on Our Campuses," *New Dimensions: The Psychology Behind the News* (June 1991): 44.

33. *Westside Community Board of Education v. Mergens*

34. Jay Sekulow and Keith Fournier, *And Nothing but the Truth* (Atlanta: Thomas Nelson, 1996), 84–5.

35. Paul Kurtz, *Toward a New Enlightenment* (New Brunswick, N.J.: Transaction, 1994).

36. Robert Holland, "Outcome-Based Education: Dumbing Down America's Schools," *Family Policy* 6, no. 5 (January 1994): 6.

37. John Ellement, "State High Court OK's Falmouth Plan to Provide Condoms in Public Schools," *The Boston Globe*, 18 July 1995.

38. H. Stephen Glenn and Jane Nelsen, *Raising Self-Reliant Children in a Self-Indulgent World* (Rocklin, Calif.: Prima Publishing & Communications, 1989), 26–7.

CHAPTER 8—TOLERANCE AND GOVERNMENT

1. Philip Yancey, "A State of Ungrace," *Christianity Today* (3 February 1997): 35.
2. Ambassador Alan Keyes, speech to Christian Coalition, Road to Victory Conference, 13 September 1997.
3. *Brigham Young University Law Review* 2 (1986): 371–404, quoted by Richard V. Pierard in "As We See It," *The Reformed Journal* 38, no. 5 (May 1988): 2–3.
4. "Commandments, Prayer, Can Stay in Ala. Courtroom," *USA Today*, 26 January 1998.
5. "National News Briefs," *Christian Times* 3, no. 9 (14 September–11 October 1997): 16.
6. Edward E. Plowman, "Broadcasters Targeted," Religion Notes, *World*, 31 January 1998, 16.
7. Jay Sekulow and Keith Fournier, *And Nothing but the Truth* (Atlanta: Thomas Nelson, 1996), 21–2.
8. Ibid., 54.
9. Edward E. Plowman, "Opening Eyes on Capitol Hill," *World*, 20 September 1997, 20.
10. Tom Minnery, "Lessons in Love," Focus on the Family *Citizen* 11, no. 6 (23 June 1997): 5.
11. The phrase "machinery of death" was used by U.S. Supreme Court justice Harry A. Blackmun, who, commenting on a recent case involving the death penalty, wrote, "From this day forward, I no longer shall tinker with the machinery of death. I feel morally and intellectually obligated simply to concede that the death penalty experiment has failed." Unfortunately, his moral and intellectual repugnance did not extend to the thirty-five million babies that have been aborted since he wrote the *Roe v. Wade* decision.
12. Reynolds Holding, "Supreme Court Rejects Appeal by Sacramento Abortion Pickets," *The San Francisco Chronicle*, 28 November 1995.

13. "Who's Intolerant?" *World*, 6 September 1997, 10.

14. Nicholas A. Christakis, et al, "Survival of Medicare Patients after Enrollment in Hospice Programs," *The New England Journal of Medicine* (18 July 1996): 174.

15. "Dr. Jack Kevorkian," www.efn.org/~ergo/Kevorkian.html, accessed January 27, 1998. This number refers to documented cases as of January 1998.

16. Michele Evans, in a letter to the editor, *Los Angeles Times*, 21 March 1997, as quoted by Matt Kaufman in "Hurry Up and Die," Focus on the Family *Citizen* (28 July 1997): 12.

17. "Bills in State Senate Promote Homosexuality, Attack the Church," *Christian Times* 3, no. 8 (10 August 10–13 September 1997): 1.

18. Brannon Howse, "The People and Agenda of Multicultural Education," *Understanding the Times,* January 1997.

19. Ibid.

20. Philip Yancey, "A State of Ungrace," *Christianity Today* (3 February 1997): 34–5.

21. John 8:31-32

22. Deborah Mendenhall, "Homosexual Anger Met with Outpouring of Christian Love," Focus on the Family *Citizen* 11, no. 6 (23 June 1997): 15.

CHAPTER 9—TOLERANCE AND SOCIETY

1. Phyllis Schlafly, "Congress Promotes Decadence through NEA," *AFA Journal* (October 1993).

2. William A. Henry III, "The Politics of Separation," *Time* (fall 1993): 75.

3. Jim Leffel, "Postmodern Impact: Literature," *The Death of Truth*, ed. Dennis McCallum (Minneapolis: Bethany House, 1996), 20.

4. Kenneth L. Woodward, "Religion: God Gets the He-Ho," *Newsweek* 126, no. 11 (11 September 1995): 76.

5. Dennis McCallum, "Evangelical Imperatives," *The Death of Truth*, ed. Dennis McCallum (Minneapolis: Bethany House, 1996), 256.

6. According to the *Advocate*, a national gay-and-lesbian magazine, as

cited by Bruce Handy in "Roll Over, Ward Cleaver," *Time* (14 April 1997): 80.

7. Robert Bork, *Slouching Towards Gomorrah* (New York: Regan Books, 1996), 144–5.

8. The belief that "all is one," a view reflected in the popular song "The Circle of Life."

9. The view that God is in everything: animals, plants, rocks, rivers, and, of course, humans.

10. "Colors of the Wind," music by Alan Menken, lyrics by Stephen Schwartz, © 1995, Wonderland Music Company, Inc., and Walt Disney Music Company.

11. David F. Wells, *No Place for Truth* (Grand Rapids: Wm. B. Eerdmans, 1993), 84.

12. Donal P. O'Mathuna, "Postmodern Impact: Health Care," *The Death of Truth,* ed. Dennis McCallum (Minneapolis: Bethany House, 1996), 20. Quotes from Dolores Krieger, *Accepting Your Power to Heal: The Personal Practice of Therapeutic Touch* (Santa Fe, N.M.: Bear & Company, 1993), 3–4, 11–13, 17.

13. Stanley Krippner, foreword to Dolores Krieger's *Accepting Your Power to Heal,* xvi.

14. Janet Mentgen and Mary Jo Trapp-Bulbrook, *Healing Touch, Level 1 Notebook* (Lakewood, Colo.: Healing Touch, 1994), 51.

15. Jeffrey Kluger, "Mr. Natural," *Time* 149, no. 19 (12 May 1997): 75.

16. Donal P. O'Mathuna, "Postmodern Impact: Health Care," 63–4.

17. This is the position of the U.S. Equal Employment Opportunity Commission (EEOC). See EEOC *Notice* N-915:022 (September 1988).

18. William T. Jarvis, "Quackery: A National Scandal," *Clinical Chemistry,* 38 (1992): 1576.

19. Walter Williams, "Elite Nazis Have Taken Over Campuses," *Dallas Morning News,* 20 February 1993.

20. Chuck Colson, "Science by Decree: The Trials of Dean Kenyon," *BreakPoint,* 19 April 1994.

21. Ibid.

22. Ibid.

23. Lee Campbell, "Postmodern Impact: Science," *The Death of Truth,* ed. Dennis McCallum (Minneapolis: Bethany House, 1996), 190.

24. Fritjof Capra, *The Tao of Physics* (Boston: Shambhala, 1991), 25.

25. Dennis McCallum, "Practical Communication Ideas," *The Death of Truth,* ed. Dennis McCallum (Minneapolis: Bethany House, 1996), 267–8.

26. Lee Campbell, "Postmodern Impact: Science," *The Death of Truth,* ed. Dennis McCallum (Minneapolis: Bethany House, 1996), 192.

CHAPTER 10—TOLERANCE AND THE CHURCH

1. J. B. Cheaney, "But Can It Save?" *World,* 20 September 1997, 34.

2. Josh McDowell and Bob Hostetler, *Right From Wrong* (Dallas: Word, 1994), 15.

3. George Barna, *What America Believes: An Annual Survey of Values and Religious Views in the United States* (Ventura, Calif.: Regal Books, 1991), 85.

4. Ted Olsen, "Many College Students Do Not Probe Beliefs," *Christianity Today* 41, no. 2 (3 February 1997): 88.

5. Gallup Poll, *PRRC Emerging Trends,* February 1992, 3.

6. "Nationline: New Bishop," *USA Today,* 12 January 1998.

7. Personal correspondence from Steve Brown, 2 June 1997.

8. The study, reported in *Theology Today* and *Vanishing Boundaries:The Religion of Mainline Protestant Baby Boomers* (Louisville, Ky.: Westminster John Knox Press, 1993), focused on five hundred baby boomers who had been confirmed in twenty-three Presbyterian churches throughout the U.S. The authors of the study considered their work representative of mainline denominations; it would be less representative of evangelical denominations.

9. Donald A. Luidens, Dean R. Hoge, and Benton Johnson, "The Emergence of Lay Liberalism among Baby Boomers," *Theology Today* 51, no. 2 (July 1994): 253.

10. Quoted by Michael S. Horton, *Beyond Culture Wars* (Chicago: Moody, 1994), 37.

11. Marcus J. Borg, "Faith and Scholarship," *Bible Review,* August 1993, 9.

12. In 1985 this group of seventy-four scholars published a summary of its "findings" amid much media fanfare in *The Five Gospels: What Did Jesus Really Say?* (1993). The seminar decreed that a mere 20 percent of the words attributed to Jesus in the Gospels were actually (or even probably) spoken by him. An excellent rebuttal to the Jesus Seminar is provided in *Jesus under Fire,* Michael J. Wilkins and J. P. Moreland, eds. (Grand Rapids: Zondervan, 1995).
13. Walt Russell, "What It Means to Me," *Christianity Today* (26 October 1992): 30.
14. Ibid., 31.
15. Gustav Niebuhr, "Southern Baptists Enact Curbs on Homosexuality," *The Washington Post,* 16 June 1993.
16. Edward E. Plowman, "Methodist Rebels," *World,* 20 December 1997, 18.
17. Larry B. Stammer, "Anglican Leader Visits L.A.," *The Los Angeles Times,* 25 May 1996.
18. Christine Wicker, "On Religion: Youths' Questions Present Opportunity for Churches," *The Dallas Morning News,* 8 July 1995.
19. Ibid.
20. Robert J. Nelson, "Tolerance, Bigotry, and the Christian Faith," *Religion in Life* 33, no. 4 (Autumn 1964).
21. Harold Netland, "Exclusivism, Tolerance, and Truth," *Evangelical Review of Theology* 12, no. 3 (July 1988): 258.
22. Wilfred Cantwell Smith, "An Attempt at Summation," in *Christ's Lordship and Religious Pluralism,* eds. Gerald H. Anderson and Thomas F. Stransky (Ann Arbor, Mich.: Books on Demand, 1981), 202.
23. Paul Knitter, *No Other Name? A Critical Survey of Christian Attitudes toward the World Religions* (Maryknoll, N.Y.: Orbis, 1985), 93.
24. Edward E. Plowman, Religion Briefs: "Canadian Rift," *World,* 20 December 1997, 17.
25. Quoted by Michael S. Horton, *Beyond Culture Wars* (Chicago: Moody, 1994), 37.
26. Peter Tze Ming Ng, "Toward a New Agenda for Religious Education in a Multicultural Society," *Religious Education* 88, no. 4 (Fall 1993): 589.

27. Charles Strohmer, personal interview with Bob Hostetler, 20 February 1997.

28. Harold Netland, "Exclusivism, Tolerance, and Truth," *Evangelical Review of Theology* 12, no. 3 (July 1988): 258.

CHAPTER 11—SHINING LIKE STARS

1. *Great Commandment Ministry Workbook* (Austin, Tex.: Intimacy, 1998), 77.

2. *Marriage in America Report,* Institute for American Values (New York, 1995).

3. *Church Youth Survey* (Richardson, Tex.: Josh McDowell Ministry, 1994).

4. "100 Things the Church Is Doing Right," *Christianity Today* (17 November 1997): 28.

5. Steve Sjogren, *Conspiracy of Kindness* (Ann Arbor, Mich.: Servant, 1993), 20–1.

6. "100 Things the Church Is Doing Right," *Christianity Today* (17 November 1997): 28.

7. Ibid., 29.

8. Ibid., 26.

9. Ibid., 24–5.

10. Chuck Colson, World Shapers Conference, Toronto, Canada, 1996.

GLOSSARY OF TERMS

1. Harold Netland, "Exclusivism, Tolerance, and Truth," *Evangelical Review of Theology* 12, no. 3 (July 1988): 258.

2. Gary W. Phillips, "Evangelical Pluralism: A Singular Problem," *Bibliotheca Sacra,* 151 (April–June 1994): 141.

3. Dennis McCallum, "Are We Ready?" *The Death of Truth,* ed. Dennis McCallum (Minneapolis: Bethany House, 1996), 13.

4. Don Closson, "Multiculturalism," 1.

5. Thomas A. Helmbock, "Insights on Tolerance," *Cross and Crescent,* summer 1996, 2.

6. Jim Leffel, "Our Old Challenge: Modernism," *The Death of Truth,* ed. Dennis McCallum (Minneapolis: Bethany House, 1996), 20.

7. Gary W. Phillips, "Evangelical Pluralism: A Singular Problem," 141.

RECOMMENDED RESOURCES

APOLOGETICS/POSTMODERNISM/TOLERANCE

Anderson, Walter Truett, ed. *The Truth about Truth.* New York: Putnam, 1995.

Bennett, William J. *The De-Valuing of America.* New York: Summit Books, 1992.

Chamberlain, Paul. *Can We Be Good Without God?* Downers Grove, Ill.: InterVarsity, 1996.

Cox, Paul. Tape series, Living in Babylon. *How to Make a Difference in a Post-Christian World,* Perspective Ministries, San Bernardino.

Evans, Tony. *Are Christians Destroying America?* Chicago: Moody, 1996.

Gaede, S. D. *When Tolerance Is No Virtue.* Downers Grove, Ill.: Inter-Varsity, 1993.

Grenz, Stanley J. *A Primer to Postmodernism.* Grand Rapids: Wm. B. Eerdmans, 1996.

Horton, Michael S. *Beyond Culture Wars.* Chicago: Moody, 1994.

McCallum, Dennis, ed. *The Death of Truth.* Minneapolis: Bethany House, 1996.

McCallum, Dennis, and Jim Leffel. Tape Series, *The Death of Truth,* The Crossroads Project. Columbus, Ohio.

McDowell, Josh, and Norm Geisler. *Love Is Always Right.* Dallas: Word, 1996.

Middleton, J. Richard, and Brian J. Walsh. *Truth Is Stranger Than It Used to Be.* Downers Grove, Ill.: InterVarsity, 1995.

Mouw, Richard J. *Distorted Truth.* New York: Harper & Row, 1989.

Newbigin, Leslie. *The Gospel in a Pluralist Society.* Grand Rapids: Wm. B. Eerdmans, 1989.

Phillips, Timothy R., and Dennis L. Okholm. *Christian Apologetics in the Postmodern World.* Downers Grove, Ill.: InterVarsity, 1995.

Sekulow, Jay, and Keith Fournier, *And Nothing but the Truth.* Atlanta: Thomas Nelson, 1996.

Sire, James W. *Chris Chrisman Goes to College.* Downers Grove, Ill.: InterVarsity, 1993.

Sproul, R. C. Tape Series, *Truth,* Ligonier Ministries, Orlando, Florida.

Sproul, R. C. Video, *Ultimate Issues: "Christ the Only Way,"* Ligonier Ministries, Orlando, Florida.

Veith, Gene Edward. *Postmodern Times.* Wheaton, Ill.: Crossway, 1994.

Watkins, William D. *The New Absolutes.* Minneapolis: Bethany House, 1996.

Zacharias, Ravi. *Deliver Us from Evil.* Dallas: Word, 1996.

MULTICULTURALISM

Bernstein, Richard. *Dictatorship of Virtue: Multiculturalism and the Battle for America's Future.* New York: Alfred A. Knopf, 1994.

D'Souza, Dinesh. *Illiberal Education.* New York, Vintage Books, 1992.

Sacks, David O., and Peter A. Thiel. *The Diversity Myth.* Oakland, Calif.: The Independent Institute, 1995.

Schlesinger, Arthur Jr. *The Disuniting of America.* New York: W. W. Norton & Co., 1992.

INDEX

ACLU 39, 76, 139
AIDS 123, 205
Aist, Dr. Jim 73
Alabama Freethought Association 139
Alice in Wonderland 71
Alliance Defense Fund 68
American Enterprise Institute 118
American Federation of Teachers 119
Anglican Church 182
Annapolis, Maryland 205
Argue, Don 48
Arizona Western College 5
Ayres, Professor David 168
Ayurvedic medicine 164

Barber, James David 64
Bates, Bruce 139
Bates, Stephen 111
Bernstein, Richard 27, 112, 119
Berry, Shannon 7
Binkley Memorial Baptist Church 181
Borg, Marcus J. 176
Borg, the 1
Bork, Judge Robert 159
Bradenton, Florida 7
British Columbia College of Teachers 45

Brookline, Massachusetts 118
Brown, David 65
Brown, Steve 174
Buddhism 60, 76
Bullard, Sara 110

California State University at Sacramento 78
Camp, Calvin J. 62
Campbell, Lee 169
Campus Crusade for Christ 74, 190
Canadian Center for Law and Justice 140
Canadian Radio/Television and Telecommunications Commission (CRT) 140
Capra, Fritjof 169
Carey, the Most Reverend George L. 182
Carleton (Ottawa) University 76
Carter, Stephen L. 59
Cartier, Onis 66
Chapel Hill, North Carolina 181
Cheaney, J. B. 173
Cheney, Lynn 113
Chesterton, G. K. 58
China 63
Chinese University of Hong Kong 120
Chopra, Deepak 164

City College of New York 123
Clitoridectomy 63
Closson, Don 18, 57
Colson, Chuck 61, 168, 169, 206
Columbus, Ohio 139
Constitution, United States 59,
115, 127
Cooney, Jim and Terri 205
Cornell University 32, 73
CORNET (Covenant
Relationships Network) 182
Creech, Pastor Jimmy 181
Croney, Art 148

D'Souza, Dinesh 118, 123
Dalai Lama 60
Dallas Baptist University 168
Dartmouth 78
Davison, Kim 205
De Russy, Candace 116
Declaration of Independence 33
Declaration on the Elimination of
All Forms of Intolerance and of
Discrimination 48
Degeneres, Ellen 159

Emory University 186
Episcopal church 174, 181
Ethical theism 33
Evans, Michele 146

Family Research Council 149
Federal Aviation Administration
39
Federal Court of Appeals 61
Fellendorf, George W. 111

Feminist Women's Health Center
144
Ferguson, Dr. David 101
Finnish Green Party 65
First Amendment (to U.S.
Constitution) 128
Fishnet Music Festival 124
Focus on the Family 141
Fournier, Keith 59, 127

Gadsden, Alabama 138
Galveston County, Texas 53
Gandhi Mandapan 48
Genovese, Eugene 118
George, Ellen 67
Glenn, H. Stephen 130
Griswold, Bishop Frank Tracy 174
Guay, Gerard Renald 140

Haire, R. M. 42
Hamilton College 25
Heidegger, Martin 65
Henry, William A., III 61, 155
Hershey, Brett 186
Hill, Dr. Frederick W. 43
Hinduism 48, 72, 164, 188
Holland, Robert 129
Holocaust, the 25
Hord, Pauline 205
Hosanna Industries 204
Houston, Texas 204
Human rights 58, 62, 63, 64

"Inclusive" version of the Bible 156
International Black Buyers and
Manufacturers Expo and
Conference 78

InterVarsity Christian Fellowship 76

Islam 48, 76, 188, 190

Ithaca, New York 73

Jackson, D. 123

Jackson, Mississippi 76, 205

Jacobs, Gwen 67

Jamison, Frank 80

Jeffrey, John 168

Jeffries, Dr. Leonard 123

Jersey City, New Jersey 39

Jesus Seminar 177

Jiang Zemin 62

Kent, Judge Samuel B. 53

Kenyon, Dean 168

Kevorkian, Jack 146

Keyes, Alan 67, 134

Kierkegaard, Søren 176, 188

King, William 122

Knitter, Paul 187

Knox, Bishop 76

Krauthammer, Charles 78

Krieger, Dolores 164

Kurtz, Paul 129

Kwanzaa 76, 78

Law of noncontradiction 72

Leffel, Jim 155

Legutko, Ryszard 43, 64

Lejeune, Jerome 145

Leo, John 25, 26

Liacos, Chief Justice Paul 130

Linkola, Pentti 65

Long, Judge James 145

Los Angeles, California 57

Love & Action 205

Lucado, Max 87

Madras, India 48

Maginnis, Robert 149

Mallon, Lucy 67

Manassas, Virginia 44

McCallum, Dennis 9, 158, 170

Medicine Hat, Alberta 140

Mensching, Gustav 47

Mims, Forest M., III 81

Minnery, Tom 141

Miss Illinois pageant 32

Miss Saigon 78

Modernism 34

Moore, Judge Roy 138

National Association of Evangelicals 48

National Center on Education and the Economy 129

National Council of Social Studies (NCSS) 110

National Endowment for the Arts (NEA) 154

National Organization of Women (NOW) 67

Nelsen, Jane 130

Nelson, J. Robert 187

Netland, Harold 187, 191

New York State Regents 24

Newkirk, Ingrid 66

Nobel Peace Prize 60

O'Mathuna, Dr. Donal 165

Oberlin College 187

Omaha, Nebraska 181

Ontario Court of Appeal 66
Operation Rescue 80
Oregon State University 176
Orwell, George 69
Osthathios, Geevarghese Mar 98
Ottawa, Quebec 66, 76
Oxford, Ohio 204

Park, Andrea 63
Paxton, Annabelle 46
People for the Ethical Treatment of Animals (PETA) 66
Phipps, Bill 188
Phoenix, Arizona 104
Pope John Paul II 145
Postmodernism 36
Presbyterian church (USA) 181
Princeton University 181
Pryce, Jonathan 78
Pullen Memorial Baptist Church 181

Quebec, Canada 78
Queens, New York 115
Quetzalcoatl 45

Rainbow Curriculum 26
Raines, Raymond 7
Raleigh, North Carolina 181
Relman, Dr. Arnold 165
Renaissance, the 34
Richter, Don C. 186
RICO (Racketeer Influenced and Corrupt Organizations Act) 80, 145
Ruivivar, Francis 78
Russell, Professor Walt 178

Sacramento, California 144, 148
Salonga, Lea 78
Salt Lake City, Utah 61
San Francisco State University 168
San Francisco, California 45
San Jose, California 45
Saunders, Debra J. 73, 75
Savater, Fernando 19, 56
Schaeffer, Dr. Francis 55
Schnell, Beverly 6
Scruggs, Scott 46
Sekulow, Jay 59, 127
Selkirk, New York 7
Serrano, Andres 39
Shanker, Albert 119
Siegel, Bernie 164
Sierra Club 65
Siler, Reverend Mahan 181
Simon, Prof. Robert 25
Smith, W. Cantwell 187
Southern Poverty Law Center 110
Sproul, R. C. 180
Stanford University 26, 46, 122
Stern, Kenneth S. 111
Stone, Oliver 160
Stott, John 96
Strohmer, Charles 190
Supreme Court 80, 127, 128, 145

Teaching Tolerance magazine 110
Therapeutic Touch 164
Through the Looking Glass 71
Trinity Western University 45
Tze Ming Ng, Peter 120, 189

U.S. Department of Health and
    Human Services 146
U.S. District Court 53
U.S. Postal Service 148
United Church of Canada 188
United Methodist Church (UMC)
    181
United Nations 47, 67, 134
University of Colorado 141
University of Connecticut 126
University of Denver 80
University of Illinois 78
University of Michigan 126
University of Pennsylvania 27,
    77, 126

Vassar 78

Veith, Gene Edward 65, 117
Voice of Calvary Ministries 205

Warner, Jerrold 5
Weil, Dr. Andrew 164
Wells, David F. 34, 161
Westside Community Board of
    Education v. Mergens 128
Wicker, Christine 186
Williamson, Marianne 164
Wood, James 47
Woodbridge, John D. 54, 102
Woodward, Kenneth 156

Yancey, Philip 149
Ypsilanti, Michigan 151

Zacharias, Ravi 50

JOSH MCDOWELL, *champion of the ongoing nationwide Right From Wrong campaign, is an internationally known speaker, author, and traveling representative for Campus Crusade for Christ. He has written more than forty books. These include* Right From Wrong, More Than a Carpenter, *and* How to Be a Hero to Your Kids. *Josh and his wife, Dottie, have four children and live in Lucas, Texas.*

BOB HOSTETLER *is a writer, editor, and speaker. He has written numerous books, including* Don't Check Your Brains at the Door, The Love Killer *(both coauthored with Josh McDowell), and* They Call Me A.W.O.L. *He and his wife, Robin, live in southwestern Ohio with their two children, Aubrey and Aaron.*

CAMPAIGN **RIGHT FROM WRONG** RESOURCES

Passing On the Truth to Our Next Generation

The Right From Wrong message, available in numerous formats, provides a blueprint for countering the culture and rebuilding the crumbling foundations of our families.

The Right From Wrong Book for Adults

Right From Wrong: What You Need to Know to Help Youth Make Right Choices
by Josh McDowell and Bob Hostetler

Our youth no longer live in a culture that teaches an objective standard of right and wrong. Truth has become a matter of taste. Morality has been replaced by individual preference. And today's youth have been affected. Fifty-seven percent of our churched youth cannot state that an objective standard of right and wrong even exists!

As the centerpiece of the Right From Wrong Campaign, this life-changing book provides you with a biblical, yet practical, blueprint for passing on core Christian values to the next generation.

Right From Wrong, Trade Paper Book
ISBN 0-8499-3604-7

The Truth Slayers Book for Youth

Truth Slayers: The Battle of Right From Wrong
by Josh McDowell and Bob Hostetler

This book, directed to youth, is written in the popular NovelPlus format. It combines the fascinating story of Brittney Marsh, Philip Milford, Jason Withers, and the consequences of their wrong choices with Josh McDowell's insights for young adults in sections called "The Inside Story."

Truth Slayers conveys the critical Right From Wrong message that challenges you to rely on God's Word as the absolute standard of truth in making right choices.

Truth Slayers, Trade Paper Book
ISBN 0-8499-3662-4

103 Questions Book for Children

103 Questions Children Ask about Right From Wrong
Introduction by Josh McDowell

"How does a person really know what is right or wrong?" "How does God decide what's wrong?" "If lying is wrong, why did God let some people in the Bible tell lies?" "What is a conscience and where does it come from?" These and 99 other questions are what kids ages 6 to 10 are asking. The *103 Questions* book equips parents to answer the tough questions kids ask about right from wrong. It also provides an easy-to-understand book that children will read and enjoy.

103 Questions, Trade Paper Book
ISBN 0-8423-4595-7

The Topsy-Turvy Kingdom Picture Book

The Topsy-Turvy Kingdom
by Dottie and Josh McDowell, with David Weiss

This fascinating story from a faraway land is written in delightful rhyme. It enables adults to teach children the importance of believing in and obeying an absolute standard of truth.

The Topsy-Turvy Kingdom, Hardcover Book for Children
ISBN 0-8423-7218-0

The Josh McDowell Family and Youth Devotionals

Josh McDowell's One Year Book of Youth Devotions by Bob Hostetler
Josh McDowell's One Year Book of Family Devotions by Bob Hostetler

These two devotionals may be used alone or together. Youth from ages 10 through 16 will enjoy the youth devotionals on their own. And they'll be able to participate in the family devotionals with their parents and siblings. Both devotionals are packed with fun-filled and inspiring readings. They will challenge you to think—and live—as "children of God without fault in a crooked and depraved generation, in which you shine like stars in the universe" (Philippians 2:15, NIV).

Josh McDowell's One Year Book of Youth Devotions
ISBN 0-8423-4301-6
Josh McDowell's One Year Book of Family Devotions
ISBN 0-8423-4302-4

Truth Matters,
Adult Video Series
ISBN 0-8499-8587-0

Setting Youth Free to Make Right
Choices, Youth Video Series
ISBN 0-8499-8585-4

Video Series for Adults and Youth

Truth Matters for You and Tomorrow's Generation Five-part adult video series featuring Josh McDowell
Setting Youth Free to Make Right Choices Five-part youth video series featuring Josh McDowell

These two interactive video series go beyond declaring what is right and wrong. They teach how to make right moral choices based on God's absolute standard of truth.

The adult series includes five video sessions, a comprehensive Leader's Guide with samplers from the five *Right From Wrong* workbooks, the *Right From Wrong* book, the *Truth Slayers* book, and an eight-minute promotional tape that will motivate adults to go through the series.

The youth series contains five video sessions, a Leader's Guide with reproducible handouts that include samplers from the *Right From Wrong* workbooks, and the *Truth Slayers* book.

The Right From Wrong Musicals for Youth

Truth Works musical by Dennis and Nan Allen
Truth Slayers musical by Steven V. Taylor and Matt Tullos

The *Truth Slayers* musical for junior high and high school students is based on the *Truth Slayers* book. The *Truth Works* musical for children is based on the *Truth Works* workbooks. As youth and children perform these musicals for their peers and families, they have a unique opportunity to tell of the life-changing message of Right From Wrong.

Each musical includes complete leader's instructions, a songbook of all music used, a dramatic script, and an accompanying soundtrack on cassette or compact disc.

Truth Works,
Musical Score
Number 318004
Truth Slayers,
Musical Score
Number 314002

CAMPAIGN RESOURCES

Workbook for Adults

Truth Matters for You and Tomorrow's Generation
Workbook and Leader's Guide
by Josh McDowell

The *Truth Matters* workbook includes 35 daily activities that help you to instill within your children and youth such biblical values as honesty, love, and sexual purity. By taking just 25 to 30 minutes each day, you will discover a fresh and effective way to teach your family how to make right choices—even in tough situations.

The *Truth Matters* workbook is designed to be used in eight adult group sessions that encourage interaction and support building. The five daily activities between each group meeting will help you and your family to make right choices a habit.

Truth Matters,
Member's Workbook
ISBN 0-8054-9834-6
Truth Matters, Leader's Guide
ISBN 0-8054-9833-8

Workbook for College Students

Out of the Moral Maze, Workbook with Leader's Instructions
by Josh McDowell

Students entering college face a culture that has lost its belief in absolutes. In today's society, truth is a matter of taste; morality, a matter of individual preference. *Out of the Moral Maze* will provide any truth-seeking collegiate with a sound moral guidance system based on God and his Word as the determining factors for making right moral choices.

Out of the Moral Maze
Member's Workbook and Leader's Instructions
ISBN 0-8054-9832-X

CAMPAIGN RESOURCES

Workbook for Junior High and High School Students

Setting You Free to Make Right Choices
Workbook and Leader's Guide
by Josh McDowell

With a Bible-based emphasis, this workbook creatively and systematically teaches your students how to determine right from wrong in their everyday lives—specifically applying the decision-making process to moral questions about lying, cheating, getting even, and premarital sex.

Through eight youth-group meetings, followed each week by five daily exercises of 20 to 25 minutes per day, your teenagers will be challenged to develop a lifelong habit of making right moral choices.

Setting You Free to Make Right Choices.
Member's Workbook ISBN 0-8054-9828-1
Setting You Free to Make Right Choices.
Leader's Guide ISBN 0-8054-9829-X

Workbooks for Children

Truth Works: Making Right Choices
Workbooks and Leader's Guide
by Josh McDowell

To pass on the truth and reclaim a generation, we must teach God's truth when our children's minds and hearts are young and pliable. Creatively developed, *Truth Works* includes two workbooks, one directed to younger children in grades one to three, the other to older children in grades four to six.

In eight fun-filled group sessions, your children will discover why such truths as honesty, justice, love, purity, self-control, mercy, and respect work to their best interests. They will see how four simple steps will help them to make right moral choices an everyday habit.

Truth Works. Younger Children's Workbook ISBN 0-8054-9831-1
Truth Works. Older Children's Workbook ISBN 0-8054-9830-3
Truth Works. Leader's Guide ISBN 0-8054-9827-3

Contact your Christian supplier to help you obtain these Right From Wrong resources and begin to make it right in your home, your church, and your community.